WHAT TO KNIT: THE TODDLER YEARS

30 gorgeous jumpers, cardigans, hats, toys & more

Nikki Van De Car

Photography by Ali Allen

Kyle Books

First published in Great Britain in 2014 by
Kyle Books
an imprint of Kyle Cathie Ltd.
67–69 Whitfield Street
London, W1T 4HF
general.enquiries@kylebooks.com
www.kylebooks.com

ISBN: 978-0-85783-185-9

Editor: Catharine Robertson
Designer: Laura Woussen
Photographer: Ali Allen
Illustrations: Ed Milsom
Design Assistant: Alison Milsom-Gilfeather
Copy Editor: Salima Hirani
Proofreader: Katie Hardwicke
Index: Helen Snaith
Production: Lisa Pinnell

Colour reproduction by Alta Image
Printed and bound in China by C&C Offset Printing Company Ltd.

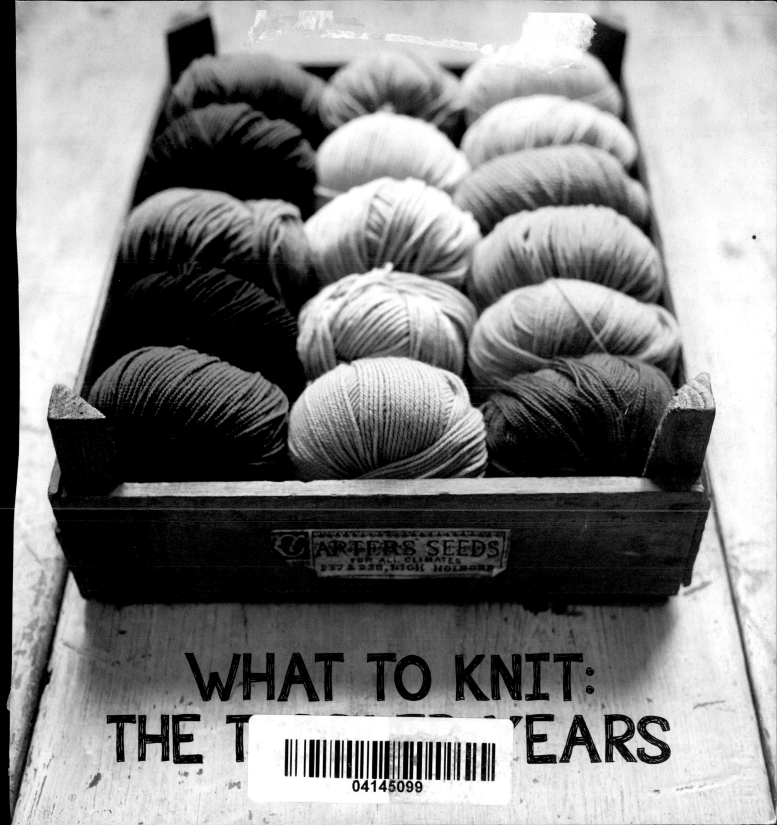

ARTERS SEEDS
FOR ALL CLIMATES

WHAT TO KNIT:
THE TODDLER YEARS

Contents

Introduction

When I was working on *What To Knit When You're Expecting*, I would hear question after question from my daughter Maile: 'Is Mommy knitting a sweater for me?' 'No, sweetie, I'm sorry.' 'That Owl and Monkey is for Maile?' 'No, my love, this Owl is not for you, it's for the book.' It was heartbreaking, and when I finished, I went a little crazy and I knitted Maile every sweater, every stuffed toy she had ever shown any interest in. Now she's a bit of a mama's knitting maniac, and I have to stash my knitting bag high overhead.

But if my very strong-willed three-year-old has taught me anything, it's that even the youngest children have profound likes and dislikes, and that they care deeply about what image they are presenting to the world. I may not, for instance, particularly appreciate Maile's t-shirt that proclaims 'My Dad is King of the Castle', but to her, it's the 'I Love My Daddy' shirt, and so will forever be a favourite. Similarly, the sweaters that she remembers Mommy making for her are treasured (and are, by the way, a very easy way to get a stubborn toddler to wear something warm on a cold day).

Those sweaters also get food, milk, juice and dirt all over them on a daily basis. I didn't quite anticipate how the level of mess would escalate as my daughter grew older, but so it has – as she plays harder, so do her clothes get harder use. And so the patterns included here are hardy enough to withstand rough play, endless snacking and regular washing, while also embodying that sense of whimsical individuality that young children love. From a little bag in which to place treasured items like the perfect rock, a dried leaf or a piece of beach glass, to overalls or a pretty lace sweater for visiting Grandma, each design in this book will appeal to the various moods, fancies and idiosyncrasies of your young child.

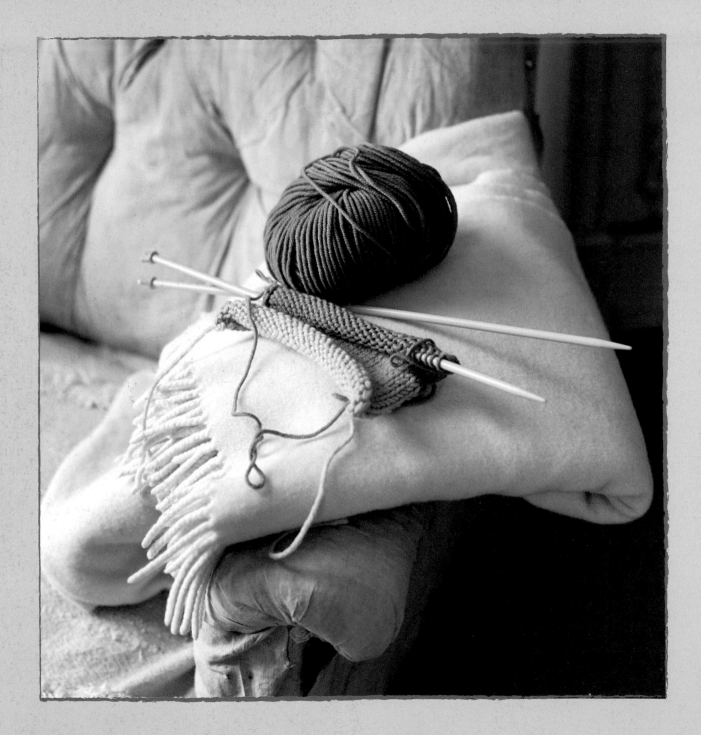

Tips &
Techniques

Sizing Information

My 3-year-old daughter fits 2T (for 2-year-olds) tops and 4T (for 4-year-olds) trousers. Sizing can never be anything other than a general guideline, and we all do the best we can. The garments in this book vary in terms of positive or negative ease – some will fit closely, others will be roomier. If you're uncertain about the fit, go up a size to be safe.

	12–18 months	18–24 months	2T	3T	4T
Chest Circumference	48cm	50.5cm	53cm	56cm	59cm
Head Circumference	39cm	39cm	41cm	41cm	43cm
Sleeve Length (from underarm to wrist)	20.5cm	21.5cm	22cm	24cm	26cm
Back Waist Length	25.5cm	26.6cm	28cm	29cm	31cm

Stitch Glossary

C3B: Cable 3 Back. Slip next 2 stitches onto cable needle and hold at back of work. Knit next stitch from left needle, then knit stitches from cable needle.

C3F: Cable 3 Front. Slip next stitch onto cable needle and hold at front of work. Knit next 2 stitches from left needle, then knit stitch from cable needle.

C4B: Cable 4 Back. Slip next 2 stitches onto cable needle and hold at back of work. Knit next 2 stitches from left needle, then knit stitches from cable needle.

C4F: Cable 4 Front. Slip next 2 stitches onto cable needle and hold at front of work. Knit next 2 stitches from left needle, then knit stitches from cable needle.

C6B: Cable 6 Back. Slip next 3 stitches onto cable needle and hold at back of work. Knit next 3 stitches from left needle, then knit stitches from cable needle.

C6F: Cable 6 Front. Slip next 3 stitches onto cable needle and hold at front of work. Knit next 3 stitches from left needle, then knit stitches from cable needle.

CC: contrast colour

CO: cast on (using the long-tail cast-on technique unless otherwise specified)

dpns: double-pointed needles

k: knit

k1tbl: knit 1 stitch through the back of the loop

k2tog: knit 2 stitches together (to decrease the number of stitches by 1)

kf&b: knit front and back – knit into the front and back of the stitch (to increase the number of stitches by 1)

m1: make 1 stitch – using your left needle, pick up the bar between the stitch on your left needle and the stitch on your right needle. Knit into the back of this (to increase the number of stitches by 1)

m1p: make 1 stitch purlwise – using your left needle, pick up the bar between the stitch on your left needle and the stitch on your right needle. Purl into the back of this (to increase the number of stitches by 1)

MC: main colour

p: purl

p2tog: purl 2 stitches together (to decrease the number of stitches by 1)

p2togtbl: purl 2 stitches together through the back of the loops (to decrease the number of stitches by 1)

pm: place marker

reverse st st: reverse stocking stitch (purl on the Right Side, knit on the Wrong Side)

RS: right side of the work

skp: slip, knit, pass (slip 1 stitch purlwise, knit the next stitch, then pass the slipped stitch over the knit stitch – 1 stitch decreased)

sl: slip (purlwise, unless otherwise specified)

sl 1-k2tog-psso: slip 1 stitch purlwise, knit 2 stitches together, pass slipped stitch over (2 stitches decreased)

ssk: slip, slip, knit (slip next 2 stitches knitwise. Slip the tip of left needle into the front of the slipped stitches, and knit them together – 1 stitch decreased)

st: stitch

sts: stitches

st st: stocking stitch (knit on the Right Side, purl on the Wrong Side)

T6B: Twist 6 Back. Slip next 3 stitches onto cable needle and hold at back of work, knit next 3 stitches from left needle, then purl stitches from cable needle.

T6F: Twist 6 Front. Slip next 3 stitches from a cable needle and hold at front of work, purl next 3 stitches from left needle, then knit stitches from cable needle.

WS: wrong side of the work

x: times (as in, repeat 3 times)

yb: yarn back – bring the working yarn to back of the knitting

yf: yarn forwards – bring the working yarn to front of the knitting

[ ] repeat the instructions inside square brackets as many times as is indicated, for example [kf&b] x 2

* repeat the instructions following/between the asterisks as indicated

General Knitting Techniques

For video tutorials for some of these techniques, go to youtube.com/user/bookskyle and search for 'What to Knit'.

Casting On

Most of the patterns in this book use long-tail cast-on. If the pattern doesn't specify a cast-on technique, long-tail is the one I had in mind, but feel free to use whichever method you like best.

1 Long-tail Cast-on:

Pull out a strand of yarn approximately three times the length of your first row. Err on the longer side to avoid having to cast on twice. Make a slipknot here, then insert your needle into the loop. *Holding the needle in your right hand, loop one strand of yarn around your left thumb, and the other strand around your left index finger. Keep your fingers stretched out, as shown. Slip the needle into the front of the loop around your thumb, then into the front of the loop around your index finger, then drop the thumb loop onto the needle. Pull tight. Repeat from * until you have cast on enough stitches.

2 Provisional Cast-on:

Using a crochet hook, chain four stitches more than need to be cast on. Break the yarn and knot the chain. Turn it over to the wrong side and insert your left knitting needle into the first or second loop on the underside of the chain. Knit this stitch onto your right needle and repeat until you have picked up and knit the number of stitches you need to cast on. When the knitting is complete, the crochet chain can be unpicked.

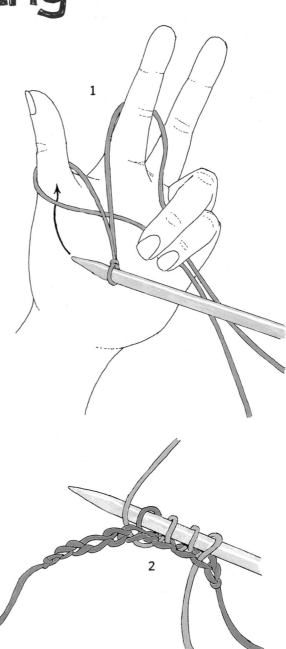

3 Backward-loop Cast-on:

Place your left index finger behind the yarn and wind it around your finger. Insert the tip of the right needle into the loop. Remove your finger and pull tight. Repeat until you have cast on enough stitches.

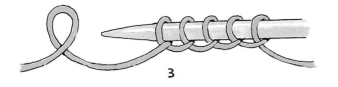

4 Cable Cast-on:

Make a slipknot and place it on the left needle. Knit into this stitch and drop the new stitch onto the left needle. *Insert your right needle in the space between the two stitches and knit a stitch from this space. Drop your new stitch onto the left needle. Repeat from * using the space between the two stitches on the left needle to cast on from until you have cast on enough stitches.

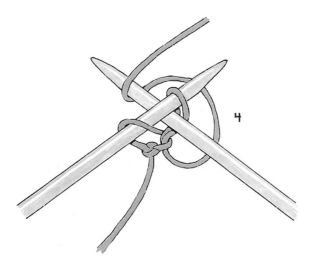

5 Garter Stitch:

When working in rows, knit all stitches, both right side and wrong side. When working in the round, alternate knit and purl rounds.

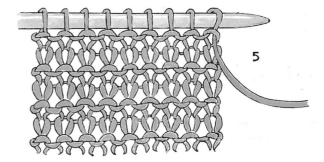

6 Stocking Stitch:

When working in rows, alternate knit and purl rows. When working in the round, knit all stitches.

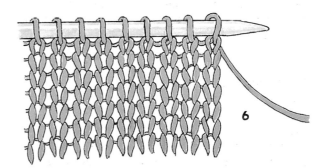

7 Picking Up Stitches:

When picking up stitches along the cast-on or cast-off edge, with right side facing insert your left needle into the 'V' of a stitch in the row just below the edge. Loop the working yarn over the needle and draw the loop through to form a stitch on the needle. Repeat until you have picked up enough stitches. When picking up stitches along the side edge, turn your work sideways. With the right side facing, and working between the first and second columns of stitches in from that edge, insert a needle between the bars between two stitches. Loop the working yarn over the needle and draw the loop through to form a stitch on the needle. Repeat until you have picked up enough stitches. Placing pins at an even distance can help you keep track of where you are.

8 I-Cord:

These instructions are for a 6-stitch i-cord. Using a double-pointed needle, cast on 6 stitches. Knit these stitches, then slide them to the opposite end of the right needle. Bring the working yarn around the back of the needle, pull it tight then, instead of turning the needle, transfer it to your left hand and knit 6 from the opposite end of the needle. Slide the stitches to the other end of the needle and repeat. Do not turn the needle at any stage, and continue working in this way until your i-cord is as long as desired.

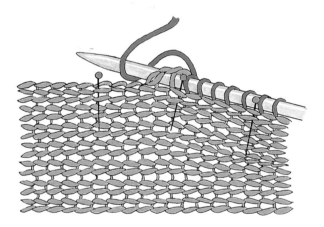

7

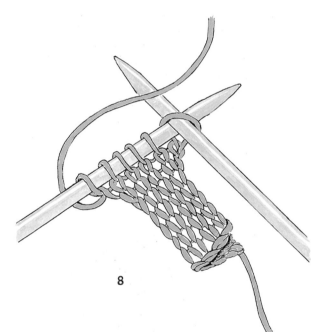

8

9 Magic Loop:

Magic loop is a technique that allows you to work in the round on a small number of stitches on a long circular needle with a flexible wire, rather than double-pointed needles. Some people prefer the technique to using double-pointed needles. None of the patterns here require an understanding of magic loop knitting, but it can be helpful (see Blocks pattern, page 112).

Once you have cast on, slide your stitches to the centre of the flexible wire. Divide them in half then, at the half-way point, pull the wire out between them into a loop. Slide the left group of the stitches onto your left needle and adjust the wire as necessary to allow the second group of stitches to rest on the wire. Bend the wire as necessary so that your right needle is free to work. Knit across the stitches on your left needle, then transfer these stitches from the right needle onto the wire. Now slide the resting group of stitches onto your left needle. Repeat to work in the round. Ensure that each time you change from working one group of stitches to the next, you pull the working yarn tight to avoid the appearance of ladders between sets of stitches.

10 Colourwork:

There are two patterns in this book that involve a bit of stranded colourwork: the Train on a Track Sweater (see page 84) and the Dandelion Sweater (see page 102). Colourwork may seem a bit intimidating at first, but it can be addictive. Many knitters recommend using a technique called 'carrying your yarn', which is a way of weaving in the colour that you aren't using into your work. I usually don't find that necessary, and the two patterns here certainly don't require it; there are no gaps between colours that are big enough to make carrying necessary. Instead, to avoid bunching your yarn when you're about to change colours, stretch out the stitches you've just worked on your right needle as far as they will comfortably go, and then pull gently on the new colour to knit the next stitch; don't pull too tightly. This will ensure that your stitches lie flat and even.

10

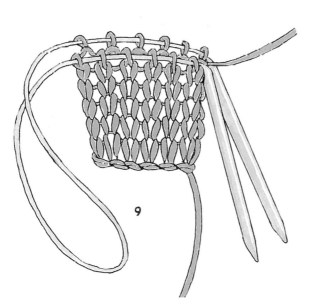

9

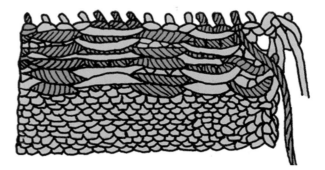

Finishing:

11 Casting Off:

Casting off begins by knitting two stitches. Then, *insert your left needle into the first stitch on your right needle that you knitted (the stitch that does not have a strand of yarn hanging from it), and pass this stitch over the second stitch and over the tip of your right needle. One stitch remains on your right needle. Knit one stitch from the left needle. Repeat from * until there are no stitches on your left needle and only one stitch remains on your right needle. Break the yarn and draw it through this remaining stitch. Pull tight.

There is a trick to keep this edge nice and stretchy: use a needle one size larger than the size you've been knitting with as your right needle. This isn't necessary as long as you don't pull too tight with the working yarn, but it does make things a little easier.

12 Mattress Stitch:

This is a fantastic seaming stitch; it's easy enough to do and creates a strong, flat and nearly invisible seam. Lay your two pieces of work flat with the right sides facing you, with the two edges that are to be joined parallel. Thread a tapestry needle with a length of yarn and insert the needle into the first row of stitches on the edge to the left, placing the needle underneath the bar between the first and second stitches in from the edge. Pull through, then place the needle under the matching bar between the first and second stitches in on the right edge. *Now insert your needle between the first and second stitches in from the left edge again, and place the needle under the bars of the next two rows. Pull through, and insert your needle under the bar of the next row up on the left edge, thereby pulling the yarn under two bars at a time, instead of just one. Repeat on the right edge from *, then work back and forth, sewing two rows at a time until the entire length is sewn. Remember to keep working between the first and second stitches in from the edge.

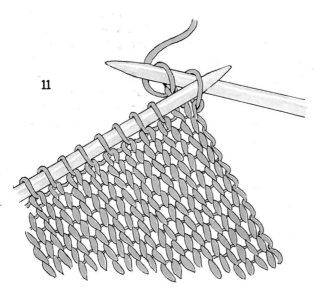

11

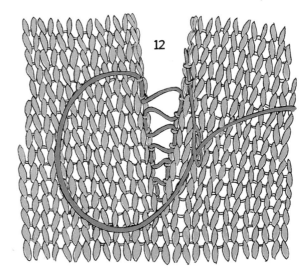

12

13 Kitchener Stitch:

Kitchener stitch grafts two equal-numbered sets of live stitches together by mimicking the way the yarn moves as it creates a knit stitch, making it appear as if there is no seam at all.

Hold two needles with the equal-numbered sets of stitches that are to be grafted parallel, with the right sides both facing up, and the working yarn attached to the upper set of stitches. Before you can begin grafting the stitches, you must prepare them for grafting.

Thread your yarn through a tapestry needle and insert the needle through the first stitch on the first knitting needle downwards, as if to purl. Pull the needle through the stitch, but leave the stitch on the knitting needle. Draw the yarn under the first knitting needle and insert your tapestry needle up through the first stitch on the second needle as if to knit. Again, leave this stitch on the knitting needle.

Now you are ready to graft the two sets of stitches together. *Insert your tapestry needle through the first stitch on the first needle upwards, as if to knit, pull the yarn through, then pull the stitch off the knitting needle. Now insert your tapestry needle through the next stitch on the first needle downwards as if to purl, and pull the yarn through. Leave this stitch on the knitting needle. Insert your tapestry needle through the first stitch on the second needle downwards as if to purl, and pull the stitch off the knitting needle as you pull the yarn through. Insert your tapestry needle through the next stitch on the second needle upwards as if to knit, and pull the yarn through. Leave this stitch on the knitting needle.

Repeat from * until all the stitches have been pulled off the needles.

14 Blocking:

My favourite method of blocking is quite aggressive and requires by far the least effort. Dunk your knitted item into a sink full of lukewarm water and swish it around a bit until you're sure it's soaked through. Very gently squeeze out most of the excess water – you don't want to wring it, but you don't need to leave it sopping wet either. Then spread it flat on a surface you won't need for a while, stretching it out to the dimensions you want it to have (but be careful not to overstretch – the garment will tell you how big it wants to be). Let it dry completely, flipping it over if you need to.

You can simply repeat this lay-flat-to-dry process with your knitted items when you've washed them after they've been worn, but be sure to pay attention to the instructions on the yarn label.

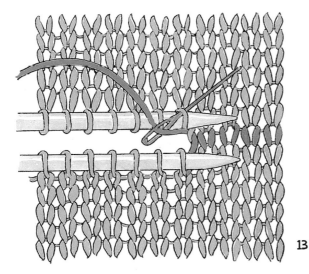

13

Chapter 1

Rough & Tumble

Ladybird on a Leaf Sweater

This playful and squishy pullover is just the thing for a budding gardener or entomologist. It is cosy while remaining light and flexible, and buttons depicting whichever bug delights you the most are sure to be a hit.

Sizes

12–18 months (18–24 months, 2T, 3T, 4T) (shown in 2T)

Materials

- 2 (2, 2, 3, 3) x 100g skeins Madelinetosh Tosh Chunky (shade: Grasshopper)
- 1 x 6mm 40cm circular needle
- 1 x pair of 6mm knitting needles
- 1 x set of 6mm double-pointed needles
- Spare yarn
- Tapestry needle
- 8 x stitch markers
- 9 x 19mm buttons

Tension

15.5 sts and 22.5 rows to 10cm over st st using 6mm needles.

Pattern

Front

Using knitting needles, CO 18 (20, 20, 22, 22) sts.

Row 1 (RS): k5, pm, k to last 5 sts, pm, k5.

Row 2 (WS) and following even rows: k to end.

Row 3: k5, sl marker, m1, k to marker, m1, sl marker, k5. 20 (22, 22, 24, 24) sts.

Row 5 (buttonhole row) (RS): k2, yf, k2tog, k1, sl marker, m1, k to marker, m1, sl marker, k1, k2tog, yf, k2. 22 (24, 24, 26, 26) sts.

Row 7: k to marker, sl marker, m1, k to marker, m1, sl marker, k to end. 24 (26, 26, 28, 28) sts.

Row 9: as Row 7. 26 (28, 28, 30, 30) sts.

Row 10: k to end.

Sizes 12–18 months and 18–24 months only

Next row (buttonhole row) (RS): k2, yf, k2tog, k1, sl marker, m1, k to marker, m1, sl marker, k1, k2tog, yf, k2. 28 (30) sts.

Next row (WS): k to marker, sl marker, p to marker, sl marker, k to end.

Sizes 2T, 3T and 4T only

Next row (RS): k to marker, sl marker, m1, k to marker, m1, sl marker, k to end. 30 (32, 32) sts.

Next row (WS): k to marker, sl marker, p to marker, sl marker, k to end.

Next row (buttonhole row) (RS): k2, yf, k2tog, k1, sl marker, m1, k to marker, m1, sl marker, k1, k2tog, yf, k2. 32 (34, 34) sts.

Next row (WS): k to marker, sl marker, p to marker, sl marker, k to end.

All Sizes

*Next row (RS): k to marker, sl marker, m1, k to marker, m1, sl marker, k to end. 30 (32, 34, 36, 36) sts.

Next row (WS): k to marker, sl marker, p to marker, sl marker, k to end. Repeat from * 6 (6, 6, 6, 7) times more until you have 42 (44, 46, 48, 50) sts, working a buttonhole every 6th (6th, 8th, 8th, 8th) row from previous buttonhole row. There should be 9 buttonhole rows in total.

Work 2 rows straight in pattern. Set Front aside.

Back

Using circular needle, CO 32 (34, 36, 38, 40) sts.

Next row (RS): k5, pm, k5 (5, 6, 6, 7), pm, k1, pm, k10 (12, 12, 14, 14), pm, k1, pm, k5 (5, 6, 6, 7), pm, k5.

Next row (WS): k to end.

*Next row (RS): k5, sl marker, m1, k to marker, [m1, sl marker, k1, sl marker, m1, k to marker] x 2, m1, sl marker, k to end. 38 (40, 42, 44, 46) sts.

Next row (WS): k to end.
Repeat from * 3 times more. 56 (58, 60, 62, 64) sts.

**Next row (RS): k5, sl marker, m1, k to marker, [m1, sl marker, k1, sl marker, m1, k to marker] x 2, m1, sl marker, k to end. 62 (64, 66, 68, 70) sts.

Next row (WS): k5, sl marker, p to last 5 sts, sl marker, k5. Repeat from ** 7 (7, 8, 9, 9) times more until you have 104 (106, 114, 122, 124) sts.

Work 2 rows straight in pattern. Break yarn.

Joining Back and Front

Sl last 5 sts (the sts away from the working yarn) of Back onto left needle. Hold Front sts so that the 1st 5 sts align with the 5 Sleeve edge sts just slipped. Holding Front sts in front, k together 5 sts from Front with the 5 sts from Sleeve, K to last 5 sts of Front, then, holding Front edge sts in front, k these together with the 5 edge sts from next Sleeve.

Removing markers as you go, k to 5th marker (start of Right Sleeve). Continuing to remove markers, sl next 32 (32, 35, 38, 38) Right Sleeve sts onto spare yarn, CO 2 sts, pm, CO 2 sts, k 36 (38, 40, 42, 44) Front sts, slip next 32 (32, 35, 38, 38) Left Sleeve sts onto spare yarn, CO 2 sts, pm, CO 2 sts, k 18 (19, 20, 21, 22) Back sts, place end-of-round marker. 80 (84, 88, 92, 96) sts.

*****Work evenly in st st for 14 (16, 18, 20, 22) rounds.

Next round: [k to 1 st before marker, m1, k1, sl marker, k1, m1] x 2, k to end of round. 84 (88, 92, 96, 100) sts. Repeat from *** once more. 88 (92, 96, 100, 104) sts. Work straight until sweater measures 27cm (28cm, 29cm, 30cm, 32cm) from cast-on edge.

****Next round: p to end.

Next round: k to end. Repeat from **** 4 times more. Cast off all sts purlwise.

Sleeves
Place Left Sleeve sts onto one dpn.

Next row (WS): attach yarn and cast off 2 sts, p to end.

Next row (RS): cast off 2 sts, k to end, pm and join to work in the round. 28 (28, 31, 34, 34) sts.

*K7 (8, 9, 10, 11) rounds.

Next round: k1, ssk, k to 3 sts before end, k2tog, k1. 26 (26, 29, 32, 32) sts. Repeat from * 3 times more. 20 (20, 23, 26, 26) sts. Work straight until sleeve measures 17.5cm (18.5cm, 19cm, 21cm, 23cm) from underarm.

****Next round:** p to end.

Next round: k to end. Repeat from ** 4 times more. Cast off all sts purlwise. Repeat with Right Sleeve sts.

Pocket
Using knitting needles, CO 17 (17, 19, 19, 21) sts. Work straight in st st for 5cm (5cm, 6cm, 6cm, 7cm), ending with a RS row.

K 5 rows.

Next row (RS): k8 (8, 9, 9, 10), yf, k2tog, k to end.

K 4 rows. Cast off all sts knitwise.

Finishing
Stitch up under the arms and weave in ends.
Sew pocket onto front of sweater as pictured.
Sew buttons opposite buttonholes.

Keaton Cardigan

Maile's friend Keaton is a rambunctious and loveably bumbling fellow who will launch headfirst into the kiddie pool. His sweater needed to give him freedom of movement while remaining funky. This cardigan is worked in reverse stocking stitch from the neck down, the sleeves are three-quarter length and the chest is shaped by a deep raglan for maximum comfort.

Sizes

12–18 months (18–24 months, 2T, 3T, 4T)
(shown in 18–24 months)

Materials

- 2 (2, 3, 3, 3) x 100g skeins Spud & Chloë Sweater (shade: 7509 Firecracker)
- 1 x 5.5mm 30cm circular needle
- 1 x set of 5.5mm double-pointed needles
- Spare yarn
- 9 x stitch markers
- 6 (7, 7, 7, 7) x 27mm buttons
- Tapestry needle

Tension

18.75 stitches and 25 rows to 10cm over st st using 5.5mm needles.

Moss Stitch pattern

Row 1: *k1, p1, repeat from * to end.

Row 2: *p1, k1, repeat from * to end.

Pattern

Using the circular needle, CO 54 (58, 60, 64, 70) sts.

Row 1 (WS): work Row 1 of moss stitch pattern.

Row 2 (RS): work Row 2 of moss stitch pattern. Repeat the last 2 rows once more, then work Row 1 once more.

Buttonhole Row 1 (RS): p1, k1, p1, yf, p2tog, *k1, p1, repeat from * to last st, k1. Work Rows 1 and 2 once more, then work Row 1 once more.

Set-up Row (RS): work first 6 sts in moss stitch, p5 (5, 5, 6, 7), pm, p2, pm, p4 (6, 6, 6, 7), pm, p2, pm, p16 (18, 18, 20, 22), pm, p2, pm, p4 (6, 6, 6, 7), pm, p2, pm, p5 (5, 5, 6, 7), work last 6 sts in moss stitch.

This gorgeous cardigan allows freedom of movement while remaining funky

All sizes

Yoke

Raglan Row 1 (WS): keeping first and last 6 sts in moss stitch, *k to marker, m1, sl marker, k2, sl marker, m1, repeat from * to last marker, k to end. 62 (66, 68, 72, 78) sts.

Raglan Row 2 (RS): keeping first and last 6 sts in moss stitch, p all sts.

Repeat Raglan Rows 1 and 2 6 times more until you have 110 (114, 116, 120, 126) sts, then work Raglan Row 1 once more.

Buttonhole Row 2 (RS): k1, p1, k1, yf, k2tog, p to last 6 sts, work last 6 sts in moss stitch.

Work Raglan Rows 1 and 2 7 times more until you have 166 (170, 172, 176, 182) sts, then work Raglan Row 1 once more.

Next row (buttonhole row) (RS): work as for Buttonhole Row 2.

Work Raglan Rows 1 and 2 1 (2, 3, 3, 3) time(s) until you have 174 (186, 196, 200, 206) sts, then work Raglan Row 1 once more.

Divide for sleeves

Next row (RS): Work first 6 sts in moss stitch, p20 (21, 22, 23, 24), remove marker, p1, pm, sl next st onto spare yarn, remove marker, sl 34 (38, 40, 40, 41) sts onto spare yarn, remove marker, sl next st onto spare yarn, p1, remove marker, p46 (48, 52, 54, 56), remove marker, p1, sl next st onto spare yarn, remove marker, sl next 34 (38, 40, 40, 41) sts onto spare yarn, remove marker, sl next st onto spare yarn, pm, p1, remove marker, p20 (21, 22, 23, 24), work in moss stitch to end.

Body

Next row (WS): keeping sts held on spare yarn in place, work 6 sts in moss stitch, k21 (22, 23, 24, 25) sts for Right Front, k48 (50, 54, 56, 58) sts for Back, k21 (22, 23, 24, 25) sts for Left Front, work in moss stitch to end. 102 (106, 112, 116, 120) sts.

Work 10 (8, 6, 6, 6) rows straight in pattern, keeping first and last 6 sts in moss stitch.

Buttonhole Row 3 (RS): k1, p1, k1, yf, k2tog, p to 1 st before marker, m1, p1, sl marker, p1, m1, p to 1 st before next marker, m1, p1, sl marker, p1, m1, p to last 6 sts, work in moss stitch to end.

*Work 13 rows straight in pattern, keeping first and last 6 sts in moss stitch.

Next row (RS): work as for Buttonhole Row 3.

Sizes 3T and 4T
Work from * once more.

Size 12–18 months
Work 2 rows straight in pattern, keeping first and last 6 sts in moss stitch.

Work 6 rows in moss stitch.
Cast off all sts in pattern.

Sizes 18–24 months and 2T
Work 11 rows straight in pattern, keeping first and last 6 sts in moss stitch.

Work 2 rows in moss stitch.

Next row (buttonhole row) (RS): k1, p1, k1, yf, k2tog, *p1, k1, repeat from * to last st, p1.

Work 3 rows in moss stitch.
Cast off all sts in pattern.

Sizes 3T and 4T
Work 2 rows straight in pattern, keeping first and last 6 sts in moss stitch.

Work 6 rows in moss stitch.
Cast off all sts in pattern.

Sleeves

Using dpns, place right sleeve sts evenly spaced across needles and attach yarn with the RS facing, pm, join to work in the round and work 5 (5, 7, 7, 9) rounds in reverse st st.

Next round: p2, p2togtbl, p to last 4 sts, p2tog, p2.

Work 5 (5, 7, 7, 9) rounds straight in pattern. Repeat from * once more.

Work 6 rounds in moss stitch.
Cast off all sts in pattern.
Repeat with Left sleeve.

Finishing

Block lightly. Weave in all ends. Attach buttons to moss stitch button band opposite buttonholes.

This fashionable
and comfortable
sweater can
stand up to
anything

Leni Sweater

Maile and her friend Leni have a game: they run in circles until they fall down – a favourite activity for toddlers everywhere! This fashionable and comfortable sweater can stand up to anything.

Sizes

12–18 months (18–24 months, 2T, 3T, 4T) (shown in 4T)

Materials

- 2 (2, 2, 2, 2) x 100g skeins Spud & Chloë Sweater (shade: 7521 Beluga) for MC
- 1 (1, 1, 2, 2) x 100g skeins Spud & Chloë Sweater (shade: 7515 Cider) for CC
- 1 x 4.5mm 40cm circular needle
- 1 x set of 4.5mm double-pointed needles
- 9 x stitch markers
- Spare yarn
- Tapestry needle
- 1 (1, 1, 2, 2) x 22mm buttons

Tension

20 sts and 24 rows to 10cm over st st using 4.5mm needles.

Stripes pattern

Each stripe of colour is worked for 7 (7, 9, 11, 13) rows/rounds by first working 7 (7, 9, 11, 13) rows/rounds of MC, then dropping MC and attaching CC and working 7 (7, 9, 11, 13) rows/rounds, in CC, and so on.

Pattern

Body

Using circular needle and MC, CO 61 (61, 65, 65, 69) sts.

K 4 rows.

Next row (buttonhole row): k2, yf, k2tog, k to end.

K 3 rows.

Raglan set-up row: k6 (6, 6, 6, 7), pm, k2, pm, k17 (17, 18, 18, 19), pm, k2, pm, k7 (7, 8, 8, 9), pm, k2, pm, k17 (17, 18, 18, 19), pm, k2, pm, k6 (6, 7, 7, 7).

Next row: k to end.

Sizes 12–18 months, 18–24 months and 2T only

Raglan row: [k to marker, m1, sl marker, k2, sl marker, m1] x 4, k to end. 69 (69, 73) sts.

Next row: k5, p to last 5 sts, k5.

Next row: k to 5 sts before end, sl last 5 sts onto a dpn. Slide sts on circular needle to other end of needle so as to join in the round. *Holding dpn in back, k together 1st st from circular needle and 1st st from dpn. Repeat from * 4 times more, pm and continue to work in the round. 64 (64, 68) sts.

*__Raglan round:__ [k to marker, m1, sl marker, k2, sl marker, m1] x 4, k to end of round. 72 (72, 76) sts.

Next round: k to end.

Repeat from * until you have 144 (152, 156) sts, working a stripe every 7 (7, 9) rounds.

Sizes 3T and 4T only
*__Raglan row:__ [k to marker, m1, sl marker, k2, sl marker, m1] x 4, k to end. 73 (77) sts.

Next row: k5, p to last 5 sts, k5.

Repeat from * once more.

Next row (buttonhole row): k2, yf, k2tog [k to marker, m1, sl marker, k2, sl marker, m1] x 4, k to end.

**__Next row:__ k5, p to last 5 sts, k5.

Next row: work Raglan row.

Repeat from ** once more.

Next row: k5, p to last 5 sts, k5.

Next row: k to 5 sts before end, sl last 5 sts onto dpn. Slide sts on circular needle to other end of needle so as to join in the round. *Holding dpn in back, k together 1st st from circular needle and 1st st from dpn. Repeat from * 4 times more, pm and join to work in the round. 100 (104) sts.

***__Raglan round:__ [k to marker, m1, sl marker, k2, sl marker, m1] x 4, k to end. 108 (112) sts.

Next round: k to end.

Repeat from *** until you have 180 (192) sts, working a stripe every 11 (13) rounds.

All sizes
Next round: k to marker, sl marker, k2, sl marker, k 21 (22, 22, 25, 27) sts, place new end-of-round marker, [k to marker, remove marker, k1, place next st on spare yarn, remove marker, place next 29 (31, 32, 38, 41) sts on spare yarn, remove marker, place next st on spare yarn, CO 4 (4, 4, 3, 3) sts using backward-loop cast-on method (see page 13), pm, CO 4 (4, 4, 3, 3) sts using backward-loop cast-on method, k1, remove marker] x 2, k to end of round. 98 (102, 104, 112, 118) sts.

Work straight in st st until you reach the end of an MC stripe. Change to CC, work 3 (3, 4, 5, 6) rounds.

Next round: [work to 1 st before side marker, m1, k1, sl marker, k1, m1] x 2, k to end. 102 (106, 108, 116, 122) sts.

Work 3 (3, 4, 5, 6) rounds. Change to MC and work MC stripe for 7 (7, 9, 11, 13) rounds. Change to CC, work 3 (3, 4, 5, 6) rounds. [Work to 1 st before side marker, m1, k1, sl marker, k1, m1] x 2, k to end. 106 (110, 112, 120, 126) sts.

Work 3 (3, 4, 5, 6) rounds. Change to MC. Work 1 round.

Next round: [work to 3 sts before side marker, cast off 3 sts, remove marker, cast off 3 sts] x 2, work to end of round. Remove end-of-round marker, work to cast-off edge. Work across 47 (49, 50, 54, 57) Back st in rows as follows:

Next row: p to end.

*__Next row:__ k2, ssk, k to last 4 sts, k2tog, k2.

Next row: p to end. Repeat from * 1 (1, 2, 3, 4) time(s) more. 43 (45, 44, 46, 47) sts. Place sts on spare yarn. Slide front sts to tip of needle with WS facing and attach yarn.

Next row: p to end.

*****Next row:*** k2, ssk, k to last 4 sts, k2tog, k2.

Next row: p to end. Repeat from * 1 (1, 2, 3, 4) time(s) more. 43 (45, 44, 46, 47) sts.

Break yarn.

Edging

With RS facing, using MC, place held Back sts on needles and k 43 (45, 44, 46, 47) sts across Back, 5 (5, 6, 6, 7) sts down decrease edge, 6 sts across cast-off edge, 5 (5, 6, 6, 7) sts up decrease edge, 43 (45, 44, 46, 47) sts across Front, 5 (5, 6, 6, 7) sts down decrease edge, 6 sts across cast-off edge, 5 (5, 6, 6, 7) sts up decrease edge, pm and join to work in the round. 118 (122, 124, 128, 134) sts on needles.

Next round: p2, pm, p39 (41, 40, 42, 43), pm, p2, pm, p5 (5, 6, 6, 7), pm, p6, pm, p5 (5, 6, 6, 7), pm, p2, pm, p39 (41, 40, 42, 43), pm, p2, pm, p5 (5, 6, 6, 7), pm, p6, pm, p5, (5, 6, 6, 7).

Next round: k to marker, sl marker, m1, k to marker, m1, sl marker, k2, sl marker, m1, k to marker, sl marker, sl 1-k2tog-psso, k to 3 sts before next marker, sl 1-k2tog-psso, sl marker, k to marker, m1, sl marker, k2, sl marker, m1, k to marker, m1, sl marker, k2, sl marker, m1, k to marker, sl marker, sl 1-k2tog-psso, k to 3 sts before next marker, sl 1-k2tog-psso, sl marker, k to marker, m1. (Stitch count unchanged.)

Next round: p to end.

Next round: k to marker, sl marker, m1, k to marker, m1, sl marker, k2, sl marker, m1, k to 3 sts before marker, sl 1-k2tog-psso, sl marker, k to marker, sl marker, sl 1-k2tog-psso, k to marker, m1, sl marker, k2, sl marker, m1, k to marker, m1, sl marker, k2, sl marker, m1, k to 3 sts before marker, sl 1-k2tog-psso, sl marker, k to marker, sl marker, sl 1-k2tog-psso, k to marker, m1. (Stitch count unchanged.)

*****Next round:*** p to end.

Next round: k to end.

Repeat from * twice more.

Cast off all sts purlwise.

Sleeves

Place Left Sleeve sts on dpns with WS facing. Attach yarn.

Next row: p to end, then pick up 3 sts from cast-off edge under arm.

Next row (RS): k to end, then pick up 3 sts from cast-off edge under arm, pm and join to work in the round. 37 (39, 40, 46, 49) sts.

If you are currently working a CC stripe, finish that stripe and work to an MC stripe, and to the end of that MC stripe.

Change to CC, and work 3 (3, 4, 5, 6) rounds.

Next round: k2, k2tog, k to last 4 sts, ssk, k2. 35 (37, 38, 44, 47) sts.

Work 3 (3, 4, 5, 6) rounds. Change to MC and work 3 (3, 4, 5, 6) rounds.

Next round: k2, k2tog, k to last 4 sts, ssk, k2. 33 (35, 36, 42, 45) sts.

Work 3 (3, 4, 5, 6) rounds. Change to CC and work 3 (3, 4, 5, 6) rounds.

Next round: k2, k2tog, k to last 4 sts, ssk, k2.
31 (33, 34, 40, 43) sts.

Work 3 (3, 4, 5, 6) rounds. Change to MC, and work 3 (3, 4, 5, 6) rounds.

Next round: k2, k2tog, k to last 4 sts, ssk, k2.
29 (31, 32, 38, 41) sts.

Work straight in st st until Sleeve measures 17.5cm (18.5cm, 19cm, 21cm, 23cm) from underarm.

***Next round:** p to end.

Next round: k to end.

Repeat from * 4 times more.

Cast off all sts purlwise.

Place Right Sleeve sts on dpns with WS facing and work as for Left Sleeve.

Finishing
Weave in ends and block lightly. Attach button(s) opposite buttonhole(s).

Russell Hoodie

Our friend Russell likes to play in the dirt and crawl around under the jungle gym. This thick and warm hoodie has a deep neck to slip easily over the head and, with its roomy front pocket, it's perfect for holding on to acorns, chalk, leaves and, perhaps, the occasional frog.

Sizes

12–18 months (18–24 months, 2T, 3T, 4T) (shown in 4T)

Materials

- 3 (3, 3, 3, 4) x 100g skeins Berroco Vintage Chunky (shade: 6175 Fennel)
- 1 x 6mm 40cm circular needle
- 1 x 5.5mm 40cm circular needle
- 1 x set of 6mm double-pointed needles
- 1 x set of 5.5mm double-pointed needles
- 8 x stitch markers
- Spare yarn
- Tapestry needle
- Crochet hook
- Toggle

Tension

14.25 sts and 19.5 rows to 10cm over st st using 6mm needles.

Pattern

CO 42 (42, 46, 50, 50) sts using provisional cast-on method (see page 12). Using the 6mm circular needle, work as follows:

Set-up row (WS): p5 (5, 6, 7, 7), pm, p2, pm, p7 (7, 7, 7, 7), pm, p2, pm, p10 (10, 12, 14, 14), pm, p2, pm, p7 (7, 7, 7, 7), pm, p2, pm, p to end.

***Next row (RS):** [k to marker, m1, sl marker, k2, sl marker, m1] x 4, k to end. 50 (50, 54, 58, 58) sts.

Next row (WS): p to end.

Repeat from * 8 (9, 9, 9, 10) times more until you have 114 (122, 126, 130, 138) sts.

Divide for sleeves

K to 1 st before marker, remove marker, k1, place next st on spare yarn, remove marker, place next 25 (27, 27, 27, 29) sts on spare yarn, remove marker, place next st on spare yarn, CO 2 (2, 3, 3, 3) sts using backward-loop cast-on method (see page 13), pm, CO 2 (2, 3, 3, 3) sts using backward-loop cast-on method, k1, remove marker, k to next marker, k1, place next st on spare yarn, remove marker, place next 25 (27, 27, 27, 29) sts on spare yarn, remove marker, place next st on spare yarn, CO 2 (2, 3, 3, 3) sts using backward-loop cast-on method, pm, CO 2 (2, 3, 3, 3) sts using backward-loop cast-on method, k1, remove marker, k to end. 68 (72, 80, 84, 88) sts.

Body

Keeping RS facing, CO 4 (6, 6, 6, 6) sts using backward-loop cast-on method, join to work in the round, k36 (38, 40, 42, 44), place end-of-round marker. 72 (78, 86, 90, 94) sts.

**Work 9 (10, 11, 12, 13) rounds straight in st st.

Next round: [k to 1 st before marker, m1, k1, sl marker, k1, m1] x 2, k to end of round. 76 (82, 90, 94, 98) sts.

Repeat from ** twice more. 84 (90, 98, 102, 106) sts.

Work 9 (10, 11, 12, 13) rounds straight in st st.
88 (94, 98, 102, 106) sts.
Piece now measures approximately 31cm (34cm, 36cm, 38cm, 41cm) from cast-on edge.

Change to 5.5mm needles. Cast off in i-cord as follows:

CO 3 sts using cable cast-on method (see page 13), *sl 3 sts from right to left needle, pull yarn around back and k2, p2tog, repeat from * until 3 sts remain, k1, p2tog, sl 2 sts onto left needle, p2tog. Break yarn.

Sleeves

Place Left Sleeve sts onto 6mm dpns with WS facing. Attach yarn.

First row: p to end, then pick up 2 (2, 3, 3, 3) sts from cast-on edge under arm. 29 (31, 32, 32, 34) sts.

Next row (RS): k to end, then pick up 2 (2, 3, 3, 3) sts from cast-on edge under arm, pm and join to work in the round. 31 (33, 35, 35, 37) sts.

Work straight in st st until sleeve measures 5cm (5cm, 5cm, 5cm, 6cm) from underarm.

Next row: k1, k2tog, k to last 3 sts, ssk, k1. 29 (31, 33, 33, 35) sts.

Work straight in st st until sleeve measures 10cm (10.5cm, 11cm, 11.5cm, 12cm) from underarm.

Next row: k1, k2tog, k to last 3 sts, ssk, k1. 27 (29, 31, 31, 33) sts.

Work straight in st st until sleeve measures 15cm (15cm, 16cm, 16cm, 18cm) from underarm.

Next row: k1, k2tog, k to last 3 sts, ssk, k1. 25 (27, 29, 29, 31) sts.

Work straight in st st until sleeve measures 20.5cm (21.5cm, 22cm, 24cm, 26cm) from underarm, then change to 5.5mm dpns. Cast off in i-cord as for bottom of Body.

Place Right Sleeve sts on 6mm dpns with WS facing and work as for Left Sleeve.

Hood

Carefully unravel provisional cast-on and place the freed sts with RS facing on 6mm circular needle.

Work 2 rows in st st.

Next row: *k3, m1, repeat from * to last 2 sts, k to end. 52 (52, 57, 62, 62) sts.

Next row: p to end.

Size 3T only
Next row: k28, m1, k to end. 58 sts.

All sizes
Work straight in st st until head measures 22cm (23cm, 24cm, 25cm, 26cm).

Next row: k26 (26, 29, 31, 31), then turn. Hold your needles parallel and graft the two sets of sts together using Kitchener stitch (see page 17).

Using 5.5mm circular needle and starting at left-bottom of neck, pick up and k18 (18, 20, 20, 22) sts along left neckline, 86 (90, 94, 98, 102) sts around hood, another 18 (18, 20, 20 22) sts along right neckline and 4 (6, 6, 6, 6) sts along bottom neck. 126 (132, 140, 144, 152) sts.

Cast off all sts in i-cord as for bottom Body and Sleeves.

Pocket

Using 6mm circular needle, CO 20 (20, 22, 22, 24) sts.

Work straight in st st for 8cm, ending with a WS row.

Next row: *k2, ssk, k to last 4 sts, k2tog, k2.
18 (18, 20, 20, 22) sts.

Next row: p to end. Repeat from * 3 (3, 4, 4, 5) times more. 12 sts.

Next row: k2, ssk, k to last 4 sts, k2tog. 10 sts. Cast off remaining sts purlwise.

Using 5.5mm circular needle and starting at bottom-right corner of pocket, pick up and k 16 sts along right edge, 10 (10, 12, 12, 14) sts along right angle, 10 sts across top, 10 (10, 12, 12, 14) sts along left angle, 16 sts down left edge and 20 (20, 22, 22, 24) sts across bottom.
82 (82, 88, 88, 94) sts.

Cast off all sts in i-cord as for bottom of Body, Sleeves and Hood.

Finishing

Sew pocket onto front of sweater as pictured, placing your sts underneath the i-cord edging so that it remains loose and three-dimensional. Stitch across bottom, sides and top, but not along the angles.

Attach yarn and, using crochet hook, chain 8cm and sew loop onto sweater as pictured. Attach toggle opposite loop.

Weave in ends and block as desired.

Overalls

This yarn behaves just like a good pair of jeans – it shrinks and fades a bit on its first wash, and softens with use. Be warned, though, that before it is washed, it bleeds heavily, so pay close attention to the finishing instructions and prepare yourself for blue fingers as you knit!

Sizes
12–18 months (18–24 months, 2T, 3T, 4T)
(shown in 18–24 months)

Materials
- 5 (5, 6, 6, 7) x 50g balls Twilleys of Stamford Denim Freedom DK (shade: 103 Denim)
- 1 x 4mm 40cm circular needle
- 2 x sets of 4mm double-pointed needles
- 3 x stitch markers
- 2 x 22mm buttons

Tension
Before washing: 20 sts and 28 rows to 10cm over st st using 4mm needles.
After washing: 20 sts and 32 rows to 10cm over st st using 4mm needles.

Pattern

Legs
Using dpns, CO 54 (58, 62, 66, 70) sts, pm and join to work in the round.

First round: p to end.

Next round: k to end. Repeat from * 6 (6, 7, 7, 8) times more.

Next round: p to end.

Work straight in st st until piece measures 24cm (27cm, 30cm, 34cm, 38cm). Break yarn and set aside.

Using second set of dpns, repeat for Second Leg. Do not break yarn.

Joining legs
Using circular needle, and removing leg markers as you go, k across 27 (29, 31, 33, 35) sts of Second Leg, CO 4 sts using backward-loop cast-on method (see page 13), k across all 54 (58, 62, 66, 70) sts of First Leg, CO 4 sts using backward-loop cast-on method, k remaining 27 (29, 31, 33, 35) sts of First Leg, place end-of-round marker and join to work in the round. 116 (124, 132, 140, 148) sts.

Work straight in st st for 14cm (16cm, 18cm, 23cm, 26cm).

Next round: p17 (19, 21, 22, 24), pm, k20 (24, 24, 26, 26), pm, p to end.

** ***Next round:*** k to end.

Next round: p to marker, k to marker, p to end of round. Repeat from ** 5 (5, 6, 6, 7) times more.

Next round: k to end. Cast off 9 (11, 12, 13, 14) sts purlwise, p8 (8, 9, 9, 10), k20 (24, 24, 26, 26), p8 (8, 9, 9, 10), cast off 26 (26, 27, 28, 29) sts purlwise, p28 (32, 36, 40, 44). Cast off all remaining sts purlwise.

Back
On the circular needle are 2 sets of sts: a set with a garter stitch border and a set without. The latter comprises sts for Back. With WS facing, attach yarn to sts for Back. 28 (32, 36, 40, 44) sts.

Work in rows as follows:

12–18 months only
***Work 9 rows in garter stitch.
Next row: k2, ssk, k to last 4 sts, k2tog, k to end. 26 sts. Repeat from *** 2 times more. 22 sts. Work 4 rows straight in st st.

Next row: work 8 sts in garter stitch, cast off 6 sts, work in garter stitch to end.

18–24 months only
***Work 5 rows in garter stitch.
Next row: k2, ssk, k to last 4 sts, k2tog, k to end. 30 sts. Repeat from *** 4 times more. 22 sts. Work 6 rows straight in garter stitch.

Next row: work 8 sts in garter stitch, cast off 6 sts, work in garter stitch to end. 16 sts.

2T only
***Work 5 rows in garter stitch.
Next row: k2, ssk, k to last 4 sts, k2tog, k to end. 34 sts. Repeat from *** 5 times more. 24 sts. Work 4 rows straight in garter stitch.

Next row: work 9 sts in garter stitch, cast off 6 sts, work in garter stitch to end.

3T only
***Work 5 rows in garter stitch.
Next row: k2, ssk, k to last 4 sts, k2tog, k to end. 38 sts. Repeat from *** 6 times more. 26 sts. Work 2 rows straight in garter stitch.

Next row: work 9 sts in garter stitch, cast off 8 sts, work in garter stitch to end.

4T only
***Work 5 rows in garter stitch.

Next row: k2, ssk, k to last 4 sts, k2tog, k to end. 42 sts. Repeat from *** 7 times more. 28 sts. Work 2 rows straight in garter stitch.

Next row: work 10 sts in garter stitch, cast off 8 sts, work in garter stitch to end.

All sizes
Work in garter stitch over the 8 (8, 9, 9, 10) Strap stitches until first Strap measures 20cm (22cm, 24cm, 26cm, 28cm) when stretched slightly. Cast off all sts. Break yarn.

Attach yarn and work second Strap as for first.

Front
With RS facing, attach yarn to sts for Front held on circular needle. 36 (40, 42, 44, 46) sts.

Keeping sts on either side of markers in garter stitch and sts between markers in st st, work straight in pattern for 8cm (9cm, 9cm, 10cm, 10cm), ending with a RS row.

K all sts for 7 (7, 8, 8, 9) rows.

Next row (buttonholes row): k 4 (4, 4, 4, 5), yf, k2tog, k to last 6 (6, 6, 6, 7) sts, k2tog, yf, k to end.

K all sts for 6 (6, 7, 7, 8) rows. Cast off all sts.

Pockets (make 2)
CO 16 (18, 20, 20, 22) sts. Work in garter stitch for 5cm (6cm, 7cm, 7cm, 8cm). Cast off all sts.

Drawstring (optional)
Using dpns, CO 2 sts and work an i-cord (see page 14) for 100cm (105cm, 110cm, 115cm, 120cm).

Finishing
Weave in ends and sew crotch seam. Sew pockets onto legs as pictured. Wash overalls and drawstring in washing machine on hot setting, then tumble dry on normal setting. Weave drawstring into waistband if desired, using a tapestry needle to insert the drawstring between stitches at evenly spaced intervals.

Pinafore Dress

This modern take on the traditional pinafore is perfect for outdoor tea parties, teddy bear picnics and cloud gazing. The buttons are sewn on both the front and the back so the straps can be easily adjusted.

Sizes

12–18 months (18–24 months, 2T, 3T, 4T) (shown in 4T)
Dress measures 35cm (38cm, 42cm, 45cm, 49cm)

Materials

- 1 (2, 2, 2, 2) x 110g skeins Dream in Color Classy (shade: Tokyo Crème) for MC
- 1 x 110g skein Dream in Color Classy (shade: Malibu Sail) for CC (note: pockets and straps are made with only the smallest amount of CC and the pattern for each size leaves enough leftover MC yarn to knit the straps and pocket with, if so desired)
- 1 x 5mm 40cm circular needle
- 8 x stitch markers
- Tapestry needle
- 4 x 18mm buttons

Tension

19 sts and 25.5 rows to 10cm over st st using 5mm needles.

Pattern

Body

Using MC, CO 90 (94, 98, 102, 108) sts, pm and join to work in the round.

P 2 rounds.

Next round: *yf, k2tog, repeat from * to end.

P 2 rounds. Work straight in st st until piece measures 7cm (7.5cm, 8cm, 9cm, 10cm).

Next round: p to end.

Next round: *yf, k2tog, repeat from * to end.

Next round: p to end.

K 3 rounds.

Next round: p to end.

Next round: *yf, k2tog, repeat from * to end.

Next round: p to end.

Skirt set-up round: k11 (11, 12, 12, 13), pm, k12 (12, 13, 13, 14), pm, k11 (12, 12, 13, 14), pm, k11 (12, 12, 13, 13), pm, k11 (12, 12, 13, 13), pm, k11 (12, 12, 13, 14), pm, k12 (12, 13, 12, 14), pm, k to end.

Perfect for
tea parties

*K 8 (9, 10, 11, 12) rounds.

Next round: [k to 1 st before marker, m1, k1, sl marker] x 8. 98 (102, 106, 110, 116) sts.

K 8 (9, 10, 11, 12) rounds.

Next round: [k1, m1, k to m, sl marker] x 8. 106 (110, 114, 118, 124) sts. Repeat from * twice more.

Work 12 (13, 10, 11, 12) rounds straight in st st. 138 (142, 146, 150, 156) sts.

P 2 rounds.

Next round: *yf, k2tog, repeat from * to end.

Next round: p to end. Cast off all sts purlwise.

Straps (make 2)
Using CC, CO 29 (31, 33, 35, 37) sts.

Next row: p to end.

Next row: k to end.

Next row: k2, *yf, k2tog, repeat from * to last st, k1.

Next row: k to end.

Next row: p to end. Cast off all sts.

Pockets (make 2)
Using CC, CO 13 (13, 13, 15, 15) sts.

**Next row:* p to end.

Next row: k2, m1, k to last 2 sts, m1, k2. 15 (15, 15, 17, 17) sts.

Repeat from * twice more. 19 (19, 19, 21, 21) sts.

Work straight in st st for 4cm (4cm, 4cm, 5cm, 5cm), ending with a RS row.

Next row: p to end.

Next row: k2, *yf, k2tog, repeat from * to last st, k1.

Cast off all sts.

Finishing
Weave in ends. Block as desired. Sew buttons on front and back as pictured and sew pockets onto front-sides of pinafore as pictured. To ensure that the pockets are level with each other, after sewing the first pocket, thread your tapestry needle with spare CC yarn and weave a line from the top of the pocket all the way across the pinafore to where the second pocket will be sewn. Repeat with bottom of pocket, then remove these lines after pockets are sewn.

Hudson Sweater

Hudson is our next-door neighbour and he's a classy guy. The woven stitch gives this strong, tweedy cotton yarn definition and keeps the sweater from sagging and the drop-shoulder involves just the tiniest bit of sewing, making this pullover both good looking and easy to knit.

Sizes

12–18 months (18–24 months, 2T, 3T, 4T) (shown in 4T)

Materials

- 2 (2, 2, 3, 3) x 100g balls Berroco Remix (shade: 3930 Smoke)
- 1 x 5mm 40cm circular needle
- 1 x set of 5mm double-pointed needles
- Tapestry needle

Tension

17 sts and 23 rows to 10cm over st st using 5mm needles.

Woven Stitch for Rounds

Round 1: k to end.

Round 2: k to end.

Round 3: *p2, k2, repeat from * to end.

Round 4: *p2, k2, repeat from * to end.

Round 5: k to end.

Round 6: k to end.

Round 7: *k2, p2, repeat from * to end.

Round 8: *k2, p2, repeat from * to end.

Woven Stitch for Rows

Row 1: k to end.

Row 2: p to end.

Row 3: *p2, k2, repeat from * to end.

Row 4: *k2, p2, repeat from * to end.

Row 5: k to end.

Row 6: p to end.

Row 7: *k2, p2, repeat from * to end.

Row 8: *p2, k2, repeat from * to end.

Pattern

Body
CO 84 (88, 92, 96, 100) sts, pm and join to work in the round.

Round 1: *k2, p2, repeat from * to end. Repeat this round 5 (5, 7, 7, 7) times more.

Begin working Woven Stitch For Rounds and work until piece measures 18cm (19cm, 21cm, 23cm, 25cm), ending with an even-numbered round.

Divide back and front
Next round: cast off 4 sts, work 38 (40, 42, 44, 46), cast off 4 sts, work to end. Leave Front sts on cord of circular needle as you work on Back.

Back
Next row: work next row of pattern, switching to corresponding row of Woven Stitch For Rows, on 38 (40, 42, 44, 46) Back sts.

Work straight in pattern until Back measures 28cm (32cm, 34cm, 38cm, 40cm), ending with a WS row.

Divide for neck
Next row (RS): work 10 (10, 10, 12, 12) sts, cast off 18 (20, 22, 20, 22), work to end.

Left Shoulder
Next row (WS): cast off 5 (5, 5, 6, 6) sts, work to end.

Next row (RS): work to end. Cast off all sts.

Right Shoulder
Sl Right Shoulder sts onto left needle and attach yarn at outside edge. With WS facing, cast off 5 (5, 5, 6, 6) sts, work to end.

Next row (RS): work 1 row.

Cast off all sts.

Front
With RS facing, attach yarn to Front sts held on cord of circular needle. Work 16 (18, 18, 20, 20), cast off 6 (4, 6, 4, 6) sts, work to end.

Right Front
With WS facing, attach yarn. *Starting with a WS row, work 3 rows.

Next row (RS): Work 2 sts, ssk, work to end.

Repeat from * 5 (7, 7, 7, 7) times more until you have 10 (10, 10, 12, 12) sts.

Work straight in pattern until Right Front measures 28cm (32cm, 34cm, 38cm, 40cm), ending with a RS row.

Right Shoulder
Next row (WS): cast off 5 (5, 5, 6, 6) sts, work to end.

Next row (RS): work to end.

Cast off all sts.

Left Front
With WS facing, attach yarn at neckline edge. *Starting with a WS row, work 3 rows.

Next row (RS): Work to last 4 sts, k2tog, work to end.

Repeat from * 5 (7, 7, 7, 7) times more until you have 10 (10, 10, 12, 12) sts.

Work straight in pattern until Left Front measures 28cm (32cm, 34cm, 38cm, 40cm), ending with a WS row.

Left Shoulder

Next row (RS): cast off 5 (5, 5, 6, 6) sts, work to end.

Next row (WS): work to end. Cast off all sts.

Sleeves

Sew shoulder seams. Using dpns, with RS facing and beginning at centre of cast-off sts at bottom of armhole, pick up and k 40 (48, 52, 56, 60) sts around one armhole, pm and join to work in the round.

**Work Woven Stitch For Rounds for 5 (5, 6, 6, 7) rounds.

Next round: Work 2 sts, ssk, work to last 4 sts, k2tog, work to end. 38 (46, 50, 54, 58) sts.

Repeat from ** 6 times more. 26 (34, 38, 42, 46) sts.

Work straight in pattern until arm measures 18.5cm (20cm, 21cm, 22cm, 24cm).

Next round: work in pattern, decreasing 6 sts evenly around sleeve. 20 (28, 32, 36, 40) sts.

Next round: *k2, p2, repeat from * to end.

Repeat this round 5 times more.

Cast off all sts in pattern.

Repeat with second sleeve.

Collar

Using the circular needle and starting at left edge of neckline, pick up and k 27 (32, 34, 36, 38) sts along left edge, 18 (20, 20, 20, 20) sts along back neck, and 27 (32, 34, 36, 38) sts along right edge. Do not pick up cast-off sts at bottom neck. 72 (84, 88 92, 96) sts. Do not join.

Next row (WS): *p2, k2, repeat from * to end.

Next row (RS): *k2, p2, repeat from * to end.

Repeat these last two rows twice more.

Cast off all sts in pattern.

Finishing

Sew edges of rib together at base of neck, with one side overlapping the other. Stitch flap down onto neckline. Weave in ends. Dunk piece in lukewarm water and lay it out flat to dry, stretching the sweater to size – avoid stretching out the ribbing.

Striped Beach Sweater

Maile's cousin Sophie had a sweater much like this that I admired, and then finagled a way to design one for Maile to wear when we all played on the beach together for a week on Cape Cod.

Sizes

12–18 months (18–24 months, 2T, 3T, 4T)
(shown in 12–18 months)

Materials

- 3 (3, 3, 4, 4) x 50g balls Debbie Bliss Eco Baby (shade: 015 Stone) for MC
- 1 x 50g ball Debbie Bliss Eco Baby (shade: 029 Denim) for CC
- 1 x 2.75mm 30cm circular needle
- 1 x 3.25mm 30cm circular needle
- 1 x set of 3.25mm double-pointed needles
- 6 x stitch markers
- Spare yarn
- Tapestry needle
- 4 (4, 4, 5, 5) x 12mm buttons

Tension

23 sts and 34 rows to 10cm over st st using 3.25mm needles.

Pattern

Using 2.75mm needles and MC, CO 89 (89, 89, 93, 93) sts.

Row 1 (WS): *k1, p1, repeat from * to last st, k1.

Row 2 (RS): *p1, k1, repeat from * to last st, p1.

Work Row 1 once more.

Next row (buttonhole row) (RS): p1, k1, yf, k2tog, *p1, k1, repeat from * to last st, p1.

Work Rows 1 and 2 once more.

Change to 3.25mm circular needle.

Raglan set-up row (WS): p35, pm, p10 (10, 10, 12, 12), pm, p32, pm, p to end.

Row 1 (RS): k1, m1, [k to marker, m1, sl marker, k1, m1] x 3, k to 1 st before end, m1, k1. 97 (97, 97, 101, 101) sts.

Row 2: p to end.

Row 3: as Row 1. 105 (105, 105, 109, 109) sts.

Row 4: drop MC (do not break), attach CC, p to end.

Row 5 (buttonhole row): using CC, k2, yf, [k to marker, m1, sl marker, m1] x 3, k to 1 st before end, m1, k1. 113 (113, 113, 117) sts.

Row 6: drop CC (do not break), pick up MC, p to end.

Row 7: using MC, work as Row 1. 121 (121, 121, 125, 125) sts.

Row 8: using MC, p to end.

Row 9: using MC, work as Row 1. 129 (129, 129, 133, 133) sts.

Row 10: using CC, p to end.

Row 11: using CC, work as Row 1. 137 (137, 137, 141, 141) sts.

Row 12: using MC, p to end.

Row 13 (buttonhole row): using MC, work as Row 5. 145 (145, 145, 149, 149) sts.

Row 14: using CC, p to end.

Row 15: using CC, work as Row 1. 153 (153, 153, 157, 157) sts.

Row 16: using MC, p to end.

Row 17: using MC, work as Row 1. 161 (161, 161, 165, 165) sts.

Row 18: using MC, p to end.

Row 19: using MC, work as Row 1. 169 (169, 169, 173, 173) sts.

Row 20: using CC, p to end.

Row 21 (buttonhole row): using CC, work as Row 5. 177 (177, 177, 181, 181) sts.

Row 22: using MC, p to end.

Row 23: using MC, work as Row 1. 185 (185, 185, 189, 189) sts.

Size 12–18 months only
Next row: using MC, p to end.

Proceed directly to Row 37.

Sizes 18–24 months, 2T, 3T and 4T
Row 24: using CC, p to end.

Row 25: using CC, work as Row 1. 193 (193, 197, 197) sts.

Row 26: using MC, p to end.

Size 18–24 months only
Proceed directly to Row 37.

Sizes 2T, 3T and 4T
Row 27: using MC, work as Row 1. 201 (205, 205) sts.

Size 2T only
Next row: using MC, p to end.

Proceed directly to Row 37.

Sizes 3T and 4T
Row 28: using CC, p to end.

Row 29 (buttonhole row): using CC, work as Row 5. 213 (213) sts.

Row 30: using MC, p to end.

Row 31: using MC, work as Row 1. 221 (221) sts.

Row 32: using MC, p to end.

Size 3T only
Proceed directly to Row 37.

Size 4T
Row 33: using MC, work as Row 1. 229 sts.

Row 34: using CC, p to end.

Row 35: using CC, work as Row 1. 237 sts.

Row 36: using MC, p to end.

All sizes
Row 37: Break CC. Using MC, k to 5 sts before end, sl next 5 sts onto dpn. Slide sts on circular needle to other end of needle so as to join in the round. *Holding dpn in back, k2tog 1st st from circular needle with the 1st st from dpn. Repeat from * 4 times more. Continuing in the round, k to marker, k28 (29, 30, 32, 34), place end-of-round marker, k to marker, place next 34 (36, 38, 44, 48) sts on spare yarn, CO 2 (2, 2, 3, 3) sts using backward-loop cast-on method (see page 13), pm, CO 2 (2, 2, 3, 3) sts using backward-loop cast-on method, k to buttonhole join, k3, place next 34 (36, 38, 44, 48) sts on spare yarn, CO 2 (2, 2, 3, 3,) sts using backward-loop cast-on method, pm, cast on 2 (2, 2, 3, 3) sts using backward-loop cast-on method, remove marker, k to end of round. 120 (124, 128, 140, 148) sts.

Body
*K 14 (16, 18, 20, 22) rounds.

Next round: [k to 1 st before side marker, m1, k 1, sl marker, k1, m1] x 2, k to end of round. 124 (128, 132, 144, 152) sts.

Repeat from * twice more. 132 (136, 140, 152, 160) sts.

Work 4 rounds straight in st st.

Change to CC, k 2 rounds.

Change to MC, k 2 rounds.

Change to CC, k 2 rounds.

Change to MC, k 2 rounds.

Change to 2.75mm circular needle.

Next round: k1, p1, repeat from * to end. Repeat previous round for 4 rounds. Cast off all sts.

Sleeves
With WS facing, place right sleeve sts on 3.25mm dpns, p to end, then pick up 2 (2, 2, 3, 3) sts from cast-on edge under arm. 36 (38, 40, 46, 50) sts.

Next row (RS): k to end, then pick up 2 (2, 2, 3, 3) sts from cast-on edge under arm, pm and join to work in the round. 38 (40, 42, 50, 54) sts.

*Work 15 (17, 19, 21, 23) rounds straight in st st.

Next round: k2, ssk, k to last 4 sts, k2tog, k2. 36 (38, 40, 46, 50) sts. Repeat from * twice more. 32 (34, 36, 44, 48) sts.

Work 4 rounds straight in st st.

*Change to CC, k 2 rows.

Change to MC, k 2 rows. Repeat from * twice more.

Change to 2.75mm circular needle.

Next round: k1, p1, repeat from * to end.

Repeat previous round for 4 rounds.

Cast off all sts.

Repeat with Left Sleeve sts.

Finishing
Block lightly. Weave in ends and stitch up under the arms. Sew buttons opposite buttonholes.

Owl & Monkey Hats

My previous book, What To Knit When You're Expecting, *featured a pair of owl and monkey pillows, echoing my daughter's ever-changing moods. Here are two hats to reflect the fact that, however much our children change as they get older, in some ways, they stay the same.*

Sizes

12–24 months (2T–3T, 4T) (shown in 12–24 months and 4T)

Materials

Monkey:
- 1 x 110g skein SweetGeorgia Superwash Worsted (shade: Bison) for MC
- 1 x 110g skein SweetGeorgia Superwash Worsted (shade: Tumbled Stone) for CC

Owl:
- 1 x 110g skein SweetGeorgia Superwash Worsted (shade: Tumbled Stone) for MC
- 1 x 110g skein SweetGeorgia Superwash Worsted (shade: Silver) for CC

Both:
- 1 x pair of 5mm knitting needles
- Stitch holder
- Tapestry needle
- Needle and thread
- Crochet hook
- Brown, white, black and orange felt squares

Tension

18.5 sts and 22 rows to 10cm over st st using 5mm needles.

Pattern

Wind MC into 2 balls. Take about 5m of 2nd ball and wind into a 3rd small ball.

Earflaps

Using 1st ball of MC, CO 3 sts.

First row: p to end.

Next row: k1, m1, k1, m1, k1. 5 sts.

*** Next row:*** p to end.

Next row: k2, m1, k to last 2 sts, m1, k2. 7 sts. Repeat from * until you have 15 (17, 19) sts.

Next row: p1, m1p, p to last st, m1p, p1. 17 (19, 21) sts.

Next row: k3, m1, k to last 3 sts, m1, k3. 19 (21, 23) sts.

Next row: p1, m1p, p to last st, m1p, p1. 21 (23, 25) sts. Place earflap onto stitch holder.

Make a 2nd earflap as for first using 2nd larger ball of MC. Do not break yarn.

Next row: k to last st of 2nd earflap. Attach CC and k last st with CC and MC held together. CO 14 (16, 16) sts using CC and the backward-loop cast-on method (see page 13).

Row 4: k18 (20, 22) MC, k2tog CC and MC, [m1, k16 (18, 18), m1] CC, ssk CC and MC, k to end MC.

Row 5: p29 (31, 35) MC, p1 MC and CC, p18 (20, 20) CC, p1 MC and CC, p to end MC.

Row 6: k17 (19, 21) MC, k2tog CC and MC, [m1, k18 (20, 20), m1] CC, ssk CC and MC, k to end MC.

Row 7: p28 (30, 34) MC, p1 MC and CC, p20 (22, 22) CC, p1 MC and CC, p to end MC.

Row 8: k16 (18, 20) MC, k2tog MC and CC, [m1, k20 (22, 22), m1] CC, ssk MC and CC, k to end MC.

Sizes 2T–3T and 4T only
Row 9: p29 (33) MC, p1 MC and CC, p24 (24) CC, p1 MC and CC, p to end MC.

Row 10: k17 (19) MC, k2tog MC and CC, [m1, k24 (24), m1] CC, ssk MC and CC, k to end MC.

All sizes
Row 9 (11, 11): p27 (28, 32) MC, p1 MC and CC, p22 (26, 26) CC, p1 MC and CC, p to end MC.

Row 10 (12, 12): k16 (17, 19) MC, k1 MC and CC, k22 (26, 26) CC, k1 MC and CC, k to end MC.

Row 11 (13, 13): as Row 9 (11, 11).

Row 12 (14, 14): k15 (16, 18) MC, k2tog MC and CC, [m1, k22 (26, 26), m1] CC, ssk MC and CC, k to end MC.

Row 13 (15, 15): p26 (29, 31) MC, p1 MC and CC, p24 (28, 28) CC, p1 MC and CC, p to end MC.

Row 14 (16, 16): k15 (16, 18) MC, k1 MC and CC, k24 (28, 28) CC, k1 MC and CC, k to end MC.

K 1st st of 1st earflap with CC and MC held together, k across 1st earflap with MC. CO 11 (11, 13) sts with MC using backward-loop cast-on method. 67 (73, 79) sts.

Body of hat
Row 1: p31 (33, 37) MC, p1 CC and MC, p14 (16, 16) CC, p1 CC and MC, p to end MC.

Row 2: k19 (21, 23) MC, k2tog CC and MC, [m1, k 14 (16, 16), m1] CC, ssk CC and MC, k to end MC.

Row 3: p30 (32, 36) MC, p1 MC and CC, p16 (18, 18) CC, p1 MC and CC, p to end MC.

Row 15 (17, 17): as Row 13 (15, 15).

Sizes 2T–3T and 4T only
Row 18: as Row 16.

Row 19: as Row 17.

All sizes
Row 16 (20, 20): k15 (16, 18), m1 MC, ssk MC and CC, k22 (26, 26) CC, k2tog MC and CC, m1, k to end MC.

Row 17 (21, 21): p27 (30, 32) MC, p1 MC and CC, p22 (26, 26) CC, p1 MC and CC, p to end MC.

Row 18 (22, 22): k16 (17, 19) MC, k1 MC and CC, k22 (26, 26) CC, k1 MC and CC, k to end MC.

Row 19 (23, 23): as Row 17 (21, 21).

Row 20 (24, 24): k16 (17, 19), m1 MC, ssk MC and CC, k20 (24, 24) CC, k2tog MC and CC, m1, k to end MC.

Row 21 (25, 25): p28 (31, 33) MC, p1 MC and CC, p20 (24, 24) CC, p1 MC and CC, p to end MC.

Sizes 2T–3T and 4T only
Row 26: k18 (20), m1 MC, ssk MC and CC, k22 (22) CC, k2tog MC and CC, m1, k to end MC.

Row 27: p32 (34) MC, p1 MC and CC, p22 (22) CC, p1 MC and CC, p to end MC.

All sizes
Row 22 (28, 28): k17 (19, 21), m1 MC, ssk MC and CC, k18 (20, 20) CC, k2tog MC and CC, m1, k to end MC.

Row 23 (29, 29): p29 (33, 35) MC, p1 MC and CC, p8 (9, 9) CC, attach 3rd small ball of MC, p2 with MC and CC held together, p8 (9, 9) CC, p1 MC and CC, p to end MC.

Row 24 (30, 30): k18 (20, 22), m1 MC, ssk MC and CC, k6 (7, 7) CC, k2tog MC and CC, m1 MC, ssk MC and CC, k6 (7,

7) CC, k2tog MC and CC, m1, k to end MC. 66 (72, 78) sts.

Row 25 (31, 31): p30 (34, 36) MC, p1 MC and CC, p6 (7, 7) CC, p1 MC and CC, p1 MC, p1 MC and CC, p6 (7, 7) CC, p1 MC and CC, p to end MC.

Row 26 (32, 32) (Note: carry CC behind MC; there's no need to attach another ball of CC): [k19 (21, 23), m1] MC, ssk MC and CC, k4 (5, 5) CC, k2tog MC and CC, [m1, k1, m1] MC, ssk MC and CC, k4 (5, 5) CC, k2tog MC and CC, [m1, k to end] MC.

Row 27 (33, 33): p31 (35, 37) MC, p6 (7, 7) MC and CC, p3 MC, p6 (7, 7) MC and CC, p to end MC.

Row 28 (34, 34): k to end MC. Break unused CC and MC yarn balls.

Work evenly in st st until hat measures 13cm (14cm, 15cm) from brim, ending with a WS row.

Next row: *k4, k2tog, repeat from * to end. 55 (60, 65) sts.

Next row: p to end.

Next row: *k3, k2tog, repeat from * to end. 44 (48, 52) sts.

Next row: p to end.

Next row: *k2, k2tog, repeat from * to end. 33 (36, 39) sts.

Next row: p to end.

Next row: *k1, k2tog, repeat from * to end. 22 (24, 26) sts.

Next row: p to end.

Next row: *k2tog, repeat from * to end. 11 (12, 13) sts.

Break yarn, leaving a long tail. Draw yarn through remaining sts and pull tight, closing the hole. Use tail to sew up seam.

Owl horns

Right Horn

Using MC and CC held together and with RS facing, pick up and k 8 sts along top of hat to one side, as pictured.

Next row: p to end.

Next row: k to end.

Next row: p to end.

Next row: k1, ssk, k to last 3 sts, k2tog, k1. 6 sts.

Next row: p to end.

Next row: k1, ssk, k2tog, k1. 4 sts.

Next row: p to end.

Next row: ssk, k2tog. 2 sts.

Next row: p2tog.

Pull yarn through final stitch.

Turn hat around so the back of the hat is facing and on the row behind the row you've just used to pick up sts for the Horn, pick up another 8 sts and work a 2nd horn directly behind the first. Sew the front and back of the horn together.

Repeat on the other side of the hat for the Left Horn.

Monkey ears

Right Ear

Using MC and CC held together and with RS facing, pick up and k 8 sts along side of hat as pictured.

Next row: p to end.

Next row: k to end.

Next row: p to end.

Next row: k1, ssk, k to last 3 sts, k2tog, k1. 6 sts.

Next row: p to end.

Next row: k1, ssk, k2tog, k1. 4 sts.

Place sts on stitch holder. Break yarn.

Turn the hat around so the back of the hat is facing, and on the row behind the row you've just used to pick up sts for the Ear, pick up another 8 sts and work a second ear directly behind the 1st. Break yarn, leaving a long tail. Graft front and back of ears together using Kitchener stitch (see page 17). Sew sides of ears together.

Repeat on the other side of the hat for the Left Ear.

Finishing

Starting at seam, using crochet hook and MC and CC held together, slip stitch evenly all along edge of earflaps and brim as follows: insert crochet hook into edge of hat, wrap and pull through. *Insert crochet hook into next st along the edge, wrap and pull through, then pull through stitch on hook. Repeat from * until you have chained 80 (90, 100) sts around edge. If desired, pick up a loop under each earflap and chain for 18cm (20cm, 22cm).

Weave in ends, wash in lukewarm water and block. Sew on felt face as pictured. Or, alternatively, sew on a kitty-cat face, or a puppy, or a panda, and so on.

Fingerless Mitts

These rustic mitts are perfect for those days when it's barely warm enough to go to the park and little hands need a bit of protection from the cold metal bars at the playground. They are sturdy and roomy enough to grow with.

Sizes

12–24 months (3T–4T)

Materials

- 1 x 50g ball Debbie Bliss Blue-Faced Leicester Aran (shade: 005 Stone)
- 1 x set of 5mm double-pointed needles

Tension

18 sts and 24 rows to 10cm over st st using 5mm needles.

Pattern (make 2)

CO 24 (27) sts. Divide evenly across dpns and join to work in the round.

Round 1: *k2, p1, repeat from * to end.

Round 2: *p1, k2, repeat from * to end.

Work these 2 rounds until piece measures 6cm (7cm) from cast-on edge, ending with Round 2.

Begin Thumbhole increases:

Round 1: k1, m1 k1, *p1, k2, repeat from * to last st, m1, p1. 26 (29) sts.

Round 2: p1, k3, *p1, k2, repeat from * to last 4 sts, p1, k1, p1, k1.

Round 3: k1, p1, m1, k1, *p1, k2, repeat from * to last 2 sts, m1, k1, p1. 28 (31) sts.

Round 4: k1, p1, k3, *p1, k2, repeat from * to last 2 sts, p1, k1.

Round 5: p1, k1, p1, m1, k1, *p1, k2, repeat from * to last 3 sts, m1, p1, k1, p1. 30 (33) sts.

Round 6: k1, p1, k1, *p1, k2, repeat from * to last 6 sts, [p1, k1] x 3.

Round 7: p1, k1, p1, k1, m1, k1, *p1, k2, repeat from *
to last 4 sts, m1, k1, p1, k1, p1. 32 (35) sts.

Thumbhole separation
Next round: k1, p1, k1, p1, k3, *p1, k2, repeat from *
to last 4 sts. Cast off 4 sts purlwise. 28 (31) sts.

Next round: Cast off 4 sts purlwise. 24 (27) sts.
Work in pattern to cast-off edge, then join to work in
the round.

Next round: *p1, k2, repeat from * to end.

Next round: *k2, p1, repeat from * to end.

Work these 2 rounds until piece measures 2cm (3cm)
from thumbhole. Cast off all sts purlwise. Weave in ends.

Chapter 2

Neat & Nice

Little Red

This sweater is as soft as can possibly be and, with a hood to cover the ears, is super cosy. Nothing could be better for visiting Grandma.

Sizes

12–18 months (18–24 months, 2T, 3T, 4T)
(shown in 12–18 months)

Materials

- 4 (4, 4, 5, 5) x 50g balls Rowan Lima (shade: 891 La Paz)
- 1 x 5.5mm 40cm circular needle
- 1 x set of 5.5mm double-pointed needles
- Spare cotton yarn in a contrast colour
- Crochet hook
- 8 x stitch markers
- 7 x 19mm buttons

Tension

20 sts and 26 rows to 10cm over st st using 5.5mm needles.

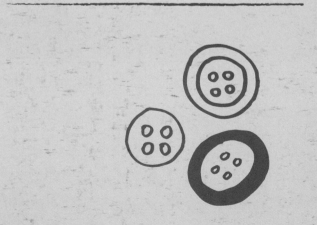

Pattern

Body

CO 57 (57, 59, 59, 61) sts using the provisional cast-on method (see page 12).

Set-up row (WS): p9 (9, 9, 9, 11), pm, p2, pm, p6 (6, 7, 7, 6), pm, p2, pm, p19 (19, 19, 19, 21), pm, p2, pm, p6 (6, 7, 7, 6), pm, p2, pm, p to end.

Row 1 (RS): [k to marker, m1, sl marker, k2, sl marker, m1] x 4, k to end. 65 (65, 67, 67, 69) sts.

Row 2 (WS): p to end.

Repeat Rows 1 and 2 11 (12, 14, 16, 17) times more until you have 153 (161, 179, 195, 205) sts.

Divide for sleeves

Next row (RS): k to marker, remove marker, k1, CO 2 sts using backward-loop cast-on method (see page 13), pm, CO 2 sts using backward-loop cast-on method, place next st on spare yarn, remove marker, place next 30 (32, 36, 40, 42) sts on spare yarn, remove marker, place next st on spare yarn, k1, remove marker, k to marker, remove marker, k1, CO 2 sts using backward-loop cast-on method, pm, CO 2 sts using backward-loop cast-on method, place next st on spare yarn, remove marker, place next 30 (32, 36, 40, 42) sts on spare yarn, remove marker, place next st on spare yarn, k1, remove marker, k to end.
97 (101, 111, 119, 125) sts.

Next row (WS): p1, *k1, p1, repeat from * to end.

Next row (RS): k1, *p1, k1, repeat from * to end. Repeat last 2 rows 1 (1, 2, 2, 2) time(s) more, then work 1 more WS row.

Next row (RS): k to end.

*Work 9 (9, 11, 11, 13) rows straight in st st.

Next row (RS): [k to 1 st before marker, m1, k1, sl marker, k1, m1] x 2, k to end. 101 (105, 115, 123, 129) sts. Repeat from * 3 times more. 113 (117, 127, 135, 141) sts.

Sizes 18–24 months and 2T only
Work 4 rows in st st.

All sizes
Next row (WS): p1, *k1, p1, repeat from * to end.

Next row (RS): k1, *p1, k1, repeat from * to end. Repeat last 2 rows once more.

Cast off all sts in pattern.

Sleeves
With WS facing, place Left Sleeve sts on dpns and attach yarn.

Working in st st, cast off 2 sts at the beginning of the next 2 rows. With RS facing, pm and join to work in the round. 28 (30, 34, 38, 40) sts.

Work straight in st st for 18cm (19cm, 20cm, 21cm, 22cm).

Next round: *k1, p1, repeat from * around. Repeat this round 3 times more.

Cast off all sts in pattern.

Repeat with Left Sleeve sts.

Hood
Carefully unravel provisional cast-on by undoing the crochet chain and pulling one st free at a time. Place each neckline st on knitting needle. 57 (57, 59, 59, 61) sts.

With RS facing, attach yarn. Work 2 rows in st st.

Next row (RS): k2 (2, 4, 4, 1), *m1, k5, repeat from * to end. 68 (68, 70, 70, 73) sts.

Size 4T only
Next row (WS): p36, p2tog, p to end.

All sizes
Work straight in st st until Hood measures 22cm (23cm, 24cm, 25cm, 26cm), ending with a WS row.

Next row: k34 (34, 35, 35, 36), then turn. Hold your needles parallel with RS facing out and graft the 2 sets of sts together using Kitchener stitch (see page 17).

Edging
Starting at lower right corner with RS facing, using circular needle, pick up and k 60 (66, 72, 78, 84) sts along right edge of cardigan, 93 (97, 101, 107, 111) sts around hood, and 60 (66, 72, 78, 84) sts along left edge of cardigan. 213 (229, 245, 263, 279) sts.

Next row (WS): p1, *k1, p1, repeat from * to end.

Next row (RS): k1, p1, k1, [yf, k2tog, work 6 (7, 8, 9, 10) sts in rib] x 6, yf, k2tog, *p1, k1, repeat from * to end.

Next row (WS): p1, *k1, p1, repeat from * to end.

Next row (RS): k1, *p1, k1, repeat from * to end.

Cast off all sts in pattern.

Finishing
Block lightly. Sew up underarms and weave in ends. Sew buttons opposite buttonholes.

Eli Vest

Maile's friend Eli is a delightful charmer who will sidle up to you with a winning smile and you'll find yourself rushing to please him. Anyone wearing this little waistcoat will seem charming and dapper, no matter whether they're throwing a tantrum or giving you a hug.

Sizes

12–18 months (18–24 months, 2T, 3T, 4T) (shown in 3T)

Materials

- 3 (3, 4, 4, 4) x 50g balls Rowan Softknit Cotton (shade: 584 Walnut)
- 1 x 4mm 40cm circular needle
- 1 x 5mm 40cm circular needle
- 1 x set of 4mm double-pointed needles
- 4 x 15mm buttons

Tension

23 sts and 44 rows to 10cm over Herringbone stitch pattern using 5mm needles.

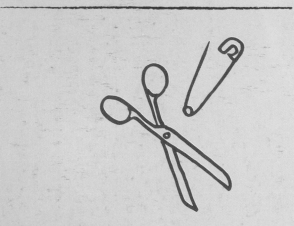

Pattern

Herringbone stitch pattern (worked over 16 rows)

Row 1 (RS): k3, *yf, sl 2, yb, k2, repeat from * to last st, k1.

Row 2 (WS): p2, *yb, sl 2, yf, p2, repeat from * to last 2 sts, p2.

Row 3: k1, yf, sl 2, yb, *k2, yf, sl 2, yb, repeat from * to last st, k1.

Row 4: p4, *yb, sl 2, yf, p2, repeat from * to end.
Work Rows 1–4 once more.

Row 9: k1, yf, sl 2, yb, *k2, yf, sl 2, yb, repeat from * to last st, k1.

Row 10: p2, *yb, sl 2, yf, p2, repeat from * to last 2 sts, p2.

Row 11: k3, *yf, sl 2, yb, k2, repeat from * to last st, k1.

Row 12: p4, *yb, sl 2, yf, p2, repeat from * to end.
Work Rows 9–12 once more.

Body

Using 4mm circular needle, CO 120 (122, 124, 132, 136) sts.

Next row (WS): *k1, p1, repeat from * to end.

Next row (RS): *k1, p1, repeat from * to end.

Work the last 2 rows 3 times more, then work 1 more WS row. Change to 5mm circular needle. Work in Herringbone stitch pattern for 10cm (11cm, 12cm, 14cm, 16cm), ending with a WS row.

Next row (RS): k2, ssk, work to last 4 sts, k2tog, k2.
118 (120, 122, 130, 134) sts.

*Keeping first and last 2 sts of each row in st st, work 7 rows straight in pattern.

Next row (RS): k2, ssk, work to last 4 sts, k2tog, k2.
116 (118, 120, 128, 132) sts.

Repeat from * 3 times more, then work 1 more WS row in pattern. 110 (112, 114, 122, 126) sts.

Next row: work 22 (23, 23, 25, 26), cast off 6 sts, work 54 (54, 56, 60, 62), cast off 6 sts, work to end.

Left Front
Leaving Back and Right Front sts resting on the cord of your circular needle, work Left Front as follows:

Next row (WS): work in pattern to last 4 sts, p2togtbl, p2.

Next row (RS): k2, ssk, work to end.

Next row (WS): work to last 4 sts, p2togtbl, p2.
19 (20, 20, 22, 23) sts.

Work 2 rows straight.

Next row: work to last 4 sts, k2tog, k2.

**Keeping first and last sts in st st, work 7 rows straight in pattern.

Next row: work to last 4 sts, k2tog, k2.

Repeat from ** 2 (2, 2, 3, 3) times more.
15 (16, 16, 17, 18) sts.

Work straight in pattern until Left Front measures 30cm (31cm, 33cm, 34cm, 36cm) from cast-on edge, ending with a WS row.

Next row: cast off 7 (8, 8, 8, 9) sts, work to end.

Next row (WS): work to end. Cast off remaining sts.

Back
Slide Back sts up to tip of circular needle with WS facing. Attach yarn. 54 (54, 56, 60, 62) sts.

Next row: p2, p2tog, work to last 4 sts, p2togtbl, p2.

Next row: k2, ssk, work to last 4 sts, k2tog, k2.

Next row: p2, p2tog, work to last 4 sts, p2togtbl, p2.
48 (48, 50, 54, 56) sts.

Work straight in pattern until Back measures 30cm (31cm, 33cm, 34cm, 46cm) from cast-on edge, ending with a WS row.

Next row: work 15 (16, 16, 17, 18) sts, cast off 18 (16, 18, 20, 20) sts, work to end.

Shape Left Shoulder
Next row (WS): cast off 7 (8, 8, 8, 9) sts, work to end.

Next row (RS): work to end. Cast off remaining sts.

70

Shape Right Shoulder

Attach yarn at Right Back Shoulder with RS facing.

Next row (RS): cast off 7 (8, 8, 8, 9) sts, work to end.

Next row (WS): work to end. Cast off remaining sts.

Right Front

Slide Right Front sts up to tip of circular needle with WS facing. Attach yarn at armpit. 22 (23, 23, 25, 26) sts.

Next row (WS): p2, p2tog, work to end.

Next row (RS): work to last 4 sts, k2tog, k2.

Next row (WS): p2, p2tog, work to end.
19 (20, 20, 22, 23) sts.

Work 2 rows straight in pattern.

Next row (RS): k2, ssk, work to end.

**Keeping first and last 2 sts of each row in st st, work 7 rows straight in pattern.

Next row: k2, ssk, work to end.

Repeat from ** 2 (2, 2, 3, 3) times more.
15 (16, 16, 17, 18) sts.

Work straight in pattern until Left Front measures 30cm (31cm, 33cm, 34cm, 36cm) from cast-on edge, ending with a WS row.

Next row: cast off 7 (8, 8, 8, 9) sts, work to end.

Next row (WS): work to end. Cast off remaining sts.

Finishing

Sew shoulder seams.

Starting at bottom corner of Left Front, with RS facing and using 4mm circular needle, pick up and k 8 sts along ribbed hem, 48 (50, 54, 56, 58) sts up to shoulder seam, 19 (19, 19, 21, 21) sts across back neck, 48 (50, 54, 56, 58) sts down to ribbed hem, 8 sts down to cast-on edge.
131 (135, 143, 149, 153) sts.

*****Next row (WS):** *p1, k1, repeat from * to last st, p1.

Next row (RS): *k1, p1, repeat from * to last st, k1.

Repeat from *** once more.

Next row (buttonhole row) (WS): work 6 (4, 6, 4, 6) sts, yf, k2tog, [work 4 (6, 6, 8, 8), yf, k2tog] x 3, work to end.

Next row (RS): *k1, p1, repeat from * to last st, k1.

Next row (WS): *p1, k1, repeat from * to last st, p1.

Next row (RS): *k1, p1, repeat from * to last st, k1.
Cast off all sts in pattern.

Armhole Edging

Starting at bottom of armhole, using dpns, with RS facing, pick up and k 42 (44, 48, 50, 52) sts around armhole. Join to work in the round.

Next round: *k1, p1, to end.

Repeat last round 4 times more. Cast off all sts in pattern.

Finishing

Weave in ends. To block, soak in lukewarm water for 5 minutes to relax the sts. Squeeze out the excess water and lay flat to dry. If desired, tack down edges of ribbed collar at shoulder seams. Sew buttons opposite buttonholes.

Olivia Cardigan

Maile's friend Olivia is a fashionista who would never go anywhere without her snazzy shades. This puff-sleeved, swingy cardigan, complete with rhinestones, is exactly her style.

Sizes

12–18 months (18–24 months, 2T, 3T, 4T)
(shown in 18–24 months)

Materials

- 1 (1, 2, 2, 2) x 100g skeins Malabrigo Arroyo (shade: 058 Borrajas)
- 1 x 3.75mm 50cm circular needle
- 1 x set of 3.75mm double-pointed needles
- Spare yarn
- Tapestry needle
- 8 x stitch markers
- 3 x 12mm buttons

Tension

24.25 sts and 29 rows to 10cm over st st using 3.75mm needles.

Pattern

Body

Using circular needle, CO 90 (90, 94, 94, 94) sts.

K 4 rows.

Next row (buttonhole row) (RS): k2, yf, k2tog, k to end.

K 2 rows.

Raglan set-up row (WS): k19 (19, 20, 20, 20), pm, k2, pm, k5, pm, k2, pm, k34 (34, 36, 36 36), pm, k2, pm, k5, pm, k2, pm, k to end.

*Puff raglan row (RS). k to marker, m1, sl marker, k2, sl marker, m1, kf&b in every st to next marker, m1, sl marker, k2, sl marker, m1, k to marker, m1, sl marker, k2, sl marker, m1, kf&b in every st to next marker, m1, sl marker, k2, sl marker, m1, k to end. 108 (108, 112, 112, 112) sts.

Next row (WS): k5, p to last 5 sts, k5. Repeat from * once more. 140 (140, 144, 144, 144) sts.

Raglan Row 1 (RS): [k to marker, m1, sl marker, k2, sl marker, m1] x 4, k to end.

Raglan Row 2 (WS): k5, p to last 5 sts, k5. Repeat Raglan Rows 1 and 2 until you have 172 (180, 184, 192, 200) sts.

Next row (buttonhole row) (RS): k2, yf, k2tog [k to marker, m1, sl marker, k2, sl marker, m1] x 4, k to end.

Next row (WS): k5, p to last 5 sts, k5. Repeat Raglan Rows 1 and 2 until you have 228 (236, 240, 256, 272) sts.

Size 12–18 months only
Next row (RS): [k to marker, remove marker, k1, place next st onto spare yarn, remove marker, place next 48 sts on spare yarn, remove marker, place next st on spare yarn, CO 4 sts using backward-loop cast-on method (see page 13), k1, remove marker] x 2, k to end. 136 sts.

Next row (WS): k to end.

Next row (buttonhole row) (RS): k2, yf, k2tog, k to end.

Next row (WS): k to end.

Size 18–24 months and 2T only
Next row (RS): k to end.

Next row (WS): k5, p to last 5 sts, k5.

Next row (RS): [k to marker, remove marker, k1, place next st onto spare yarn, remove marker, place next 50 sts on spare yarn, remove marker, place next st onto spare yarn, CO 4 sts using backward-loop cast-on method, k1, remove marker] x 2, k to end. 140 (144) sts.

Next row (WS): k to end.

Next row (buttonhole row) (RS): k2, yf, k2tog, k to end.

Next row (WS): k to end.

Size 3T only
Next row (RS): k to end.

Next row (WS): k5, p to last 5 sts, k5.

Next row (RS): [k to marker, remove marker, k1, place next st onto spare yarn, remove marker, place next 54 sts on spare yarn, remove marker, place next st onto spare yarn, CO 6 sts using backward-loop cast-on method, k1, remove marker] x 2, k to end. 156 sts.

Next row (WS): k to end.

Next row (buttonhole row) (RS): k2, yf, k2tog, k to end.

Next row (WS): k to end.

Size 4T only
Next row (RS): k to end.

Next row (WS): k5, p to last 5 sts, k5.

Next row (RS): [k to marker, remove marker, k1, place next st onto spare yarn, remove marker, place next 58 sts on spare yarn, remove marker, place next st onto spare yarn, CO 6 sts using backward-loop cast-on method, k1, remove marker] x 2, k to end. 164 sts.

Next row (WS): k to end.

Next row (buttonhole row) (RS): k2, yf, k2tog, k to end.

Next row (WS): k to end.

All sizes
Next row (RS): k10 (9, 11 11, 13), pm, k23, pm, [k8 (10, 10, 14, 12), pm, k23, pm] x 3, k to end.

Next row (WS): k5, p to last 5 sts, k5.

Row 1 (RS): k to marker, sl marker, [k8, k2tog, yf, k1, p1,

k1, yf, skp, k8, sl marker, k to marker, sl marker] x 3, k8, k2tog, yf, k1, p1, k1, yf, skp, k8, sl marker, k to end.

Row 2 (WS): k5, p to marker, sl marker, [p7, p2togtbl, p2, yf, k1, yb, p2, p2tog, p7, sl marker, p to marker, sl marker] x 3, p7, p2togtbl, p2, yf, k1, yb, p2, p2tog, p7, sl marker, p to last 5 sts, k to end.

Row 3: k to marker, sl marker, [k6, k2tog, k1, yf, k2, p1, k2, yf, k1, skp, k6, sl marker, k to marker, sl marker] x 3, k6, k2tog, k1, yf, k2, p1, k2, yf, k1, skp, k6, sl marker, k to end.

Row 4: k5, p to marker, sl marker, [p5, p2togtbl, p3, yb, p1, k1, p1, yb, p3, p2tog, p5, sl marker, p to marker, sl marker] x 3, p5, p2togtbl, p3, yb, p1, k1, p1, yb, p3, p2tog, p5, sl marker, p to last 5 sts, k to end.

Row 5: k to marker, sl marker, [k4, k2tog, k2, yf, k3, p1, k3, yf, k2, skp, k4, sl marker, k to marker, sl marker] x 3, k4, k2tog, k2, yf, k3, p1, k3, yf, k2, skp, k4, sl marker, k to end.

Row 6: k5, p to marker, sl marker, [p3, p2togtbl, p4, yb, p2, k1, p2, yb, p4, p2tog, p3, sl marker, p to marker, sl marker] x 3, p3, p2togtbl, p4, yb, p2, k1, p2, yb, p4, p2tog, p3, p to last 5 sts, k to end.

Row 7: k to marker, sl marker, [k2, k2tog, k3, yf, k4, p1, k4, yf, k3, skp, k2, sl marker, k to marker, sl marker] x 3, k2, k2tog, k3, yf, k4, p1, k4, yf, k3, skp, k2, sl marker, k to end.

Row 8: k5, p to marker, sl marker, [p1, p2togtbl, p5, yb, p3, k1, p3, yb, p5, p2tog, p1, sl marker, p to marker, sl marker] x 3, p1, p2togtbl, p5, yb, p3, k1, p3, yb, p5, p2tog, p1, sl marker, p to last 5 sts, k to end.

Row 9: k to marker, sl marker, [k2tog, k4, yf, k5, p1, k5, yf, k4, skp, sl marker, k to marker, sl marker] x 3, k2tog, k4, yf, k5, p1, k5, yf, k4, skp, sl marker, k to end.

Row 10: k5, p to marker, sl marker, [p11, k1, p11, sl marker, p to marker, sl marker] x 3, p11, k1, p11, sl marker, p to last 5 sts, k to end.

Row 11 (increase row): k to marker, m1, sl marker, [k11, p1, k11, sl marker, m1, k to marker, m1, sl marker] x 3, k11, p1, k11, sl marker, m1, k to end. 144 (148, 152, 164, 172) sts.

Row 12: As row 10. Repeat Rows 1–12 3 (3, 4, 4, 5) times more. 168 (172, 184, 196, 212) sts.

K 9 rows. Cast off all sts.

Sleeves

With WS facing, place Left Sleeve sts on dpns and attach yarn. Working in st st, cast off 2 (2, 2, 3, 3) sts at beginning of the next 2 rows. 46 (48, 48, 50, 54) sts. With RS facing, pm and join to work in the round.

Work 3 (3, 4, 4, 5) rounds straight in st st.

Next round: k2 (0, 0, 2, 2), *k2tog, k2. Repeat from * to end. 35 (36, 36, 38, 41) sts.

Next round: k13 (14, 14, 15, 16), [k2tog] x 4, k to end. 31 (32, 32, 34, 37) sts.

Next round: p to end.

Next round: k to end.

Next round: p to end.

Next round: k to end. Cast off all sts purlwise. Repeat with Right Sleeve sts.

Finishing

Sew underarms and weave in ends. Block generously, stretching and lengthening the lace skirt. Sew on buttons opposite buttonholes.

Sandy Vest

I knitted this vest during Hurricane Sandy in October 2012, while the winds shook the windows and trees and the lights flickered on and off. It is exactly the bulky, cosy vest I wanted Maile to be wearing on such a day.

Sizes

12–18 months (18–24 months, 2T, 3T, 4T) (shown in 2T)

Materials

- 1 (2, 2, 3, 3) x 100g balls Rowan Alpaca Chunky (shade: 078 Heron)
- 1 x 10mm 60cm circular needle
- 1 x set of 10mm double-pointed needles
- Tapestry needle
- Stitch marker

Tension

11 sts and 14 rows to 10cm over st st using 10mm needles.

Moss Stitch Rib Rounds

Round 1: *k1, p1, repeat from * to end.

Round 2: k to end.

Pattern

Using circular needle, CO 54 (56, 58, 60, 62) sts, pm and join to work in the round.

Round 1: p to end.

Round 2: k to end.

Repeat from * 3 times more.

Work in moss stitch rib until piece measures 16cm (17cm, 19cm, 21cm, 23cm), ending with Round 1.

Cast off 5 (6, 5, 6, 7) sts, k22 (22, 24, 24, 24), cast off 5 (6, 5, 6, 7) sts. Leaving Front sts on cord of circular needle, work Back in rows as follows:

Next row (RS): k1 to last 4 sts, k2tog, k2.
21 (21, 23, 23, 23) sts.

Next row (WS): *p1, k1, repeat from * to last 4 sts, p2togtbl, work 2 in pattern. 20 (20, 22, 22, 22) sts.

Keeping your sts in pattern, work the last 2 rows once more. 18 (18, 20, 20, 20) sts.

Work straight in moss stitch rib until back measures 27.5cm (28.5cm, 30cm, 31cm, 33cm) from cast-on edge, ending with a WS row.

Next row: k4 (4, 5, 5, 5), cast off 10 sts, k to end.

A bulky, cosy vest
for blustery days

Leaving Right Shoulder sts on needles, shape Left Shoulder as follows:

Next row (WS): cast off 2 (2, 3, 3, 3), p to end.

Next row (RS): k to end. Cast off all sts.

Attach yarn to Right Shoulder sts with RS facing.

Next row (RS): cast off 2 (2, 3, 3, 3), k to end.

Next row (WS): p to end.Cast off all sts.

Front
Attach yarn with RS facing. 22 (22, 24, 24, 24) sts.

Next row (RS): k to last 4 sts, k2tog, work 2 in pattern.
21 (21, 23, 24, 24) sts.

Next row (WS): work in moss stitch rib to last 4 sts, p2togtbl, work 2 in pattern. 20 (20, 22, 22, 22) sts.

Next row (RS): work 7 (7, 8, 8, 8) in pattern, cast off 6 sts, work in pattern to last 4 sts, k2tog, work 2 in pattern.

Leaving Right Shoulder sts on cord of circular needle, work Left Shoulder as follows:

Next row (WS): work 1 row in pattern.

Next row (RS): work 2 in pattern, ssk, work in pattern to end. 5 (5, 6, 6, 6) sts.

Keeping your stitches in pattern, work last 2 rows once more, then work straight in pattern until Left Shoulder measures 27.5cm (28.5cm, 30cm, 31cm, 33cm) from cast-on edge, ending with a RS row. 4 (4, 5, 5, 5) sts.

Next row (WS): cast off 2 (2, 3, 3, 3), p to end.

Next row (RS): k to end. Cast off all sts.

With RS facing, attach yarn to Right Shoulder sts. Work Right Shoulder as follows:

Next row: work 2 in pattern, ssk, work in pattern to end. 6 (6, 7, 7, 7) sts.

Next row (WS): work 2 in pattern, p2tog, work in pattern to end. 5 (5, 6, 6, 6) sts.

Next row (RS): work 1 row in pattern.

Keeping your sts in pattern, work last 2 rows once more, then work straight in pattern until Right Shoulder measures 27.5cm (28.5cm, 30cm, 31cm, 33cm) from cast-on edge, ending with a WS row. 4 (4, 5, 5, 5) sts.

Next row (RS): cast off 2 (2, 3, 3, 3), k to end.

Next row (WS): p to end. Cast off all sts.

Finishing

Sew shoulder seams.

Using circular needle and starting at back-right neckline, pick up and k 48 (52, 56, 60, 64) sts around neckline, pm and join to work in the round.

Round 1: p to end.

Round 2: k to end.

Cast off all sts purlwise.

Using dpns and starting at left underarm, pick up and k 22 (24, 26, 28, 30) sts around armhole, pm and join to work in the round.

Round 1: p to end.

Round 2: k to end.

Cast off all sts purlwise.

Repeat with Right Armhole.

Weave in all ends and block, stretching the vest vertically but not horizontally, as alpaca tends to sag sideways a bit and the ribbing will stretch on its own.

Joseph Cardigan

Maile's cousin, Joe, is an irresistibly charming, completely irrepressible flirt, and he seems to put no effort into it whatsoever. This cardigan is similarly unfussy. With almost no shaping, it eases a raglan yoke into a rounded neckline.

Sizes

12–18 months (18–24 months, 2T, 3T, 4T) (shown in 3T)

Materials

- 3 (3, 3, 3, 4) x 50g balls Rowan Baby Merino Silk DK (shade: 681 Zinc)
- 1 x 4mm 80cm circular needle
- 2 x stitch holders or spare yarn
- 10 x stitch markers
- 5 (6, 6, 6, 6) x 15mm buttons
- Tapestry needle
- Needle & thread

Tension

21 sts and 28 rows to 10cm over st st using 4mm needles.

Pattern

Sleeves (make 2)

CO 32 (34, 34, 36, 36) sts.

Work 14 rows in garter stitch.

Work straight in st st until piece measures 20cm (21cm, 21.5cm, 23.5cm, 25.5cm), ending with a WS row.

Cast off 4 sts at beginning of the next 2 rows. Place Sleeve on stitch holder.

Body

CO 116 (124, 128, 136, 140) sts.

Work 6 rows in garter stitch.

Next row (buttonhole row) (RS): k3, yf, k2tog, k to end.

Work 6 rows in garter stitch.

Next row (WS): k29 (31, 32, 34, 35), pm, k58 (62, 64, 68, 70), pm, k to end.

Starting with a RS row, work 8 rows in st st, keeping 1st and last 7 sts in garter stitch.

Next row (buttonhole row) (RS): k3, yf, k2tog, [k to 3 sts before marker, ssk, k1, sl marker, k1, k2tog] x 2, k to end. 114 (122, 126, 134, 138) sts.

*Work 15 rows straight in pattern.

Next row (buttonhole row) (RS): k3, yf, k2tog, [k to 3 sts before marker, ssk, k1, sl marker, k1, k2tog] x 2, k to end. 112 (120, 124, 132, 136) sts.

Repeat from * once more, so you have 4 buttonholes, ending with a buttonhole row. 110 (118, 122, 130, 134) sts.

Size 18–24 months and 2T only
Work 4 more rows in pattern.

Size 3T only
Work 6 more rows in pattern.

Size 4T only
Work 8 more rows in pattern.

All sizes
Next row (WS): k7, p18 (20, 21, 23, 24), cast off 8 sts, p44 (48, 50, 54, 56), cast off 8 sts, p to last 7 sts, k to end.

Yoke
Next row (RS): k first 24 (26, 27, 29, 30) sts of Body, pm, k1, k 1st st of left Sleeve, pm, k to 1 st before end of left Sleeve, pm, k1, k 1 st from back of Body, pm, k to 1 st before end of back of Body, pm, k1, k 1st st of right Sleeve, pm, k to 1 st before end of right Sleeve, pm, k1, k 1 st from right Body, pm, k to end of Body.
142 (154, 158, 170, 174) sts.

Next row (WS): **k7, p to last 7 sts, k7.

Next row (RS): [k to 2 sts before marker, ssk, slm, k2, slm, k2tog] x 4, k to end. 134 (146, 150, 162, 166) sts.

Repeat from ** 1 (2, 2, 3, 3) times more, continuing to work buttonhole at 16-row intervals. 126 (130, 134, 138, 142) sts.

Starting with a WS row, work 5 rows in garter stitch.

Next row (RS): k9, *k2tog, k2, repeat from * to last 9 sts,

k9. 99 (102, 105, 108, 111) sts.

K 5 rows in garter stitch.

Next row (RS): k9, *k2, k2tog, repeat from * to last 10 (9, 8, 7, 10) sts, k10 (9, 8, 7, 10). 79 (81, 83, 85, 88) sts.

Starting with a WS row, work 5 rows in garter stitch.

Next row (RS): k8 (9, 8, 9, 8), *k2tog, k2, repeat from * to last 7 (8, 7, 8, 8) sts, k7 (8, 7, 8, 8). 63 (65, 66, 68, 70) sts.

Size 12–18 months only
Cast off all sts.

Sizes 18–24 months and 2T only
Next row (WS): k to end.

Next row (buttonhole row) (RS): work as per previous buttonhole row.

Starting with a WS row, k 2 rows.

Cast off all sts.

Size 3T only
Starting with a WS row, k 2 rows.

Cast off all sts.

Size 4T only
Cast off all sts.

Finishing
Block lightly. Sew sleeve seams. Weave in ends. Attach buttons opposite buttonholes.

Train on a Track Sweater

Maile has a book that we spent an entire afternoon reading, over and over. It's not very long and it's very repetitive and it inspired this sweater. Train on the track, clickety clack.

Sizes

12–18 months (18–24 months, 2T, 3T, 4T)
(shown in 18–24 months)

Materials

- 2 (2, 3, 3, 4) x 50g balls Debbie Bliss Rialto 4-ply (shade: 06 Stone) for MC
- 1 x 50g ball Debbie Bliss Rialto 4-ply (shade: 03 Black) for CC1
- 1 x 50g ball Debbie Bliss Rialto 4-ply (shade: 28 Tangerine) for CC2
- 1 x 50g ball Debbie Bliss Rialto 4-ply (shade: 18 Teal) for CC3
- 1 x 3.5mm 40cm circular needle
- 1 x set of 3.5mm double-pointed needles
- Spare yarn
- Tapestry needle

Tension

28 sts and 39 rows to 10cm over st st using 3.5mm needles.

Railroad Track pattern

Round 1: *k1 CC1, k1 MC, repeat from * around.
Round 2: k to end CC1.
Rounds 3–5: as Round 1.
Round 6: as Round 2.
Round 7: as Round 1.

Pattern

Body

Using MC and circular needle, CO 136 (144, 152, 160, 168) sts, pm and join to work in the round.

Next round: *k1, p1, repeat from * to end.

Repeat last round until piece measures 3cm from cast-on edge.

K 3 rounds.

Attach CC1 and work Railroad Track pattern once. Break CC1. Wind a small amount (about 10m) of CC1 into a smaller ball and set it aside.

Using MC, work straight in st st until piece measures 18cm (19cm, 20cm, 22cm, 23cm) from hem.

Next round: k28 (30, 30, 32, 33), break yarn and place next 12 (12, 16, 16, 18) sts on spare yarn, reattach yarn, k56 (60, 60, 64, 66), break yarn and place next 12 (12, 16, 16,

18) sts on spare yarn, reattach yarn and k to end of round. Set aside, leaving working yarn attached.

Sleeves (make 2)

Using dpns and a new ball of MC, CO 40 (44, 48, 52, 56) sts, pm and join to work in the round.

Next round: *k1, p1, repeat from * to end.

Repeat last round until piece measures 3cm.

K 3 rounds.

Attach CC1 and work Railroad Track pattern once. Break CC1.

Using MC, k 2 rounds.

Next round: k1, m1, k to last st, m1, k1. 42 (46, 50, 54, 58) sts.

*K 4 (4, 6, 6, 8) rounds.

Next round: k1, m1, k to last st, m1, k1. 44 (46, 52, 56, 60) sts.

Repeat from * 4 times more. 52 (56, 60, 64, 68) sts.

Work straight until Sleeve measures 21cm (22cm, 23cm, 25cm, 27cm) from bottom of cuff.

Next round: k to last 6 (6, 8, 8, 9) sts.

Place next 12 (12, 16, 16, 18) sts on spare yarn. Break yarn and set aside.

Yoke

Join Body and Sleeves. Return to body piece.

Next round: k28 (30, 30, 32, 33) sts to sleeve break of body, k across 40 (44, 44, 48, 50) sts of 1st sleeve, k across 56 (60, 60, 64, 66) sts of front of body, k across 40 (44, 44, 48, 50) sts of 2nd sleeve, k28 (30, 30, 32, 33) sts to end-of-round marker on body. 192 (208, 208, 224, 232) sts.

K 4 (4, 6, 6, 8) rounds.

Attach CC1 and work Railroad Track pattern once. Do not break CC1.

K 2 (2, 3, 3, 4) rounds.

Next round: *k1, k2tog, repeat from * to last 0 (1, 1, 2, 1) st(s), k to end. 128 (139, 139, 150, 155) sts.

Next round: k to end.

Sizes 18–24 months and 2T only
Next round: [k27, m1] x 5, k to end. 144 sts.

Size 3T only
Next round: [k23, k2tog] x 6. 144 sts.

Size 4T only
Next round: [k31, m1] x 5. 160 sts.

All sizes
K 2 (1, 2, 2, 3) round(s).

Work Train pattern
Note: When working locomotive, attach that smaller ball of CC1 and use it, carrying it loosely back to the beginning of the locomotive on subsequent rounds. On Rounds 4 and 5, use the larger ball of CC1, then resume using the smaller ball on Rounds 6–9.

All sizes
Round 1: k2 MC, k2 CC1, *k4 MC, k2 CC1, k8 MC, k2 CC1, repeat from * to last 12 sts, k4 MC, k2 CC1, k6 MC.

Size 12–18 months only
Round 2: [k5 CC2, k2 CC3, k5 CC2, k4 MC, k5 CC3, k2 CC2, k5 CC3, k4 MC] x 2.
Locomotive: k2 CC1, k2 CC3, k2 CC1, k2 CC2, k2 CC1, k2

CC3, k4 MC, k5 CC2, k2 CC3, k5 CC2, k4 MC, k5 CC3, k2 CC2, k5 CC3, k4 MC, k5 CC2, k2 CC3, k5 CC2, k4 MC.

Sizes 18–24 Months, 2T and 3T only

Round 2: [k5 CC2, k2 CC3, k5 CC2, k4 MC, k5 CC3, k2 CC2, k5 CC3, k4 MC] x 2, k5 CC2, k2 CC3, k5 CC2, k4 MC.
Locomotive: k2 CC1, k2 CC3, k2 CC1, k2 CC2, k2 CC1, k2 CC3, k4 MC, k5 CC2, k2 CC3, k5 CC2, k4 MC, k5 CC3, k2 CC2, k5 CC3, k4 MC, k5 CC2, k2 CC3, k5 CC2, k4 MC.

Size 4T only

Round 2: [k5 CC2, k2 CC3, k5 CC2, k4 MC, k5 CC3, k2 CC2, k5 CC3, k4 MC] x 3.
Locomotive: k2 CC1, k2 CC3, k2 CC1, k2 CC2, k2 CC1, k2 CC3, k4 MC, k5 CC2, k2 CC3, k5 CC2, k4 MC, k5 CC3, k2 CC2, k5 CC3, k4 MC, k5 CC2, k2 CC3, k5 CC2, k4 MC.

All sizes

Round 3: as Round 2.

Size 12–18 months only

Round 4: [k5 CC2, k2 CC3, k5 CC2, k4 CC1, k5 CC3, k2 CC2, k5 CC3, k4 CC1] x 2.

Locomotive: k2 CC1, k2 CC2, k2 CC1, k2 CC3, k2 CC1, k2 CC2, k4 CC1, k5 CC2, k2 CC3, k5 CC2, k4 CC1, k5 CC3, k2 CC2, k5 CC3, k4 MC, k5 CC2, k2 CC3, k5 CC2, k4 CC1.

Sizes 18–24 months, 2T and 3T only

Round 4: [k5 CC2, k2 CC3, k5 CC2, k4 CC1, k5 CC3, k2 CC2, k5 CC3, k4 CC1] x 2, k5 CC2, k2 CC3, k5 CC2, k4 CC1.

Locomotive: k2 CC1, k2 CC2, k2 CC1, k2 CC3, k2 CC1, k2 CC2, k4 CC1, k5 CC2, k2 CC3, k5 CC2, k4 CC1, k5 CC3, k2 CC2, k5 CC3, k4 MC, k5 CC2, k2 CC3, k5 CC2, k4 CC1.

Size 4T only

Round 4: [k5 CC2, k2 CC3, k5 CC2, k4 CC1, k5 CC3, k2 CC2, k5 CC3, k4 CC1] x 3.

Locomotive: k2 CC1, k2 CC2, k2 CC1, k2 CC3, k2 CC1, k2 CC2, k4 CC1, k5 CC2, k2 CC3, k5 CC2, k4 CC1, k5 CC3, k2 CC2, k5 CC3, k4 MC, k5 CC2, k2 CC3, k5 CC2, k4 CC1.

All Sizes

Round 5: as Round 4.

Round 6: as Round 2.

Round 7: as Round 2. Break CC2 and CC3.

Round 8: k73 (89, 89, 105) MC, k2 CC1, k to end of round MC.

Round 9: k72 (88, 88, 88, 104) MC, k4 CC1, k to end of round MC.

Next round: using MC, k to end.

Next round: *k2, k2tog, repeat from * to end. 96 (108, 108, 108, 120) sts.

K 1 (1, 2, 2, 3) round(s).

Work Railroad Track pattern once. Break CC1.

Next round: using MC, k to end.

Next round: *k3, k2tog, repeat from * to last 1 (3, 3, 3, 0) st(s), k to end. 77 (87, 87, 87, 96) sts.

Sizes 12–18 months, 18–24 months, 2T and 3T only

Increase 1 st on next round. 78 (88, 88, 88) sts.

Size 4T only

Next round: k to end.

All sizes

Next round: *k1, p1, repeat from * to end.

Repeat last round for 2cm.

Cast off all sts in pattern.

Finishing

Place held underarm stitches on needles and graft top and bottom held underarm stitches together using Kitchener stitch (see page 17). Weave in ends.

To block, soak in lukewarm water for at least 5 minutes to relax sts. Stretch flat to dry.

Kalen Cardigan

My cousin's son Kalen will sleep through anything, is happy to be held by anyone and is generally the most easy-going child I've ever met. His name is Irish for 'warrior', and this cable-knit is for him, even if he is an entirely peaceful soul.

Sizes

12–18 months (18–24 months, 2T, 3T, 4T) (shown in 2T)

Materials

- 2 (2, 3, 3, 3) x 100g skeins Skacel Simpliworsted (shade: 064 Totally Taupe)
- 1 x pair of 6mm knitting needles
- 2 x stitch markers
- Cable needle
- Spare yarn
- Tapestry needle
- 5 x 25mm buttons

Tension

16 sts and 20 rows to 10cm over st st using 6mm needles.

Pattern

Back

CO 45 (47, 49, 51, 53) sts.

Next row (WS): *k1, p1, repeat from * to last st, k1.

Next row (RS): *p1, k1, repeat from * to last st, p1.

Repeat last 2 rows once more, then work 1 more WS row.

Next row (RS): p to end.

Next row (WS): k to end.

Repeat last 2 rows until piece measures 17cm (18cm, 19cm, 21cm, 23cm) from cast-on edge, ending with a RS row.

Cast off 3 sts at the beginning of the next 2 rows. 39 (41, 43, 45, 47) sts.

Next row (WS): k2, ssk, k to last 4 sts, k2tog, k2.

Next row (RS): p to end.

Repeat last 2 rows 8 (9, 9, 10, 10) times more, then work 1 more decrease row. Break yarn and place remaining 19 (19, 21, 21, 23) sts on spare yarn.

Right Front

CO 17 (19, 21, 23, 25) sts.

Next row (WS): *k1, p1, repeat from * to last st, k1.

Next row (RS): *p1, k1, repeat from * to last st, p1.
Repeat last 2 rows once more, then work 1 more WS row.

Sizes 12–18 months and 18–24 months only
Row 1: p1, k6, p1, k2, sl 1, p6 (8).

Row 2: k6 (8), sl 1, p2, k1, p6, k1.

Row 3: p1, C6B, p1, C3F, p6 (8).

Row 4: k6 (8), p3, k1, p6, k1.

Sizes 2T, 3T and 4T only
Row 1: p1 (1, 2), k6, p1 (1, 2), C4B, k2, p7 (9, 9).

Row 2: k7 (9, 9), p6, k1 (1, 2), p6, k1 (1, 2).

Row 3: p1 (1, 2), C6B, p1 (1, 2), k2, C4F, p7 (9, 9).

Row 4: k7 (9, 9), p6, k1 (1, 2), p6, k1 (1, 2).

All sizes
Repeat Rows 1–4 until piece measures 17cm (18cm, 19cm, 21cm, 23cm) from cast-on edge, ending with a RS row.

Maintaining cable pattern established, work Raglan decreases as follows (**Note:** as your work decreases, you will no longer be able to work all the cable sts as written. Work those sts in st st, keeping 3 armpit sts in reverse st st):

Next row (WS): cast off 3 sts, work to end in pattern.

Next row (RS): work to end in pattern.

Next row (WS): k2, ssk, work to end in pattern.

Next row (RS): work to end in pattern.

Repeat last 2 rows 8 (9, 9, 10, 10) times more, then work one more decrease row. Break yarn and place remaining 4 (5, 7, 8, 10) sts on spare yarn.

Left Front

CO 17 (19, 21, 23, 25) sts.

Next row (WS): *k1, p1, repeat from * to last st, k1.

Next row (RS): *p1, k1, repeat from * to last st, p1.

Repeat last 2 rows once more, then work 1 more WS row.

Sizes 12–18 months and 18–24 months only
Row 1: p6 (8), sl 1, k2, p1, k6, p1.

Row 2: k1, p6, k1, p2, sl 1, k6 (8).

Row 3: p6 (8), C3B, p1, C6F, p1.

Row 4: k1, p6, k1, p3, k6 (8).

Sizes 2T, 3T and 4T only
Row 1: p7 (7, 9), k2, C4F, p1 (1, 2), k6, p1 (1, 2).

Row 2: k1 (1, 2), p6, k1 (1, 2), p6, k7 (9, 9).

Row 3: p7 (7, 9), C4B, k2, p1 (1, 2), C6F, p1 (1, 2).

Row 4: k1 (1, 2), p6, k1 (1, 2), p6, k7 (9, 9).

All sizes
Repeat Rows 1–4 until piece measures 17cm (18cm, 19cm, 21cm, 23cm) from cast-on edge, ending with a WS row.

Maintaining cable pattern established, work Raglan decreases as follows (**Note:** as your work decreases, you will no longer be able to work all the cable sts as written. Work those sts in st st, keeping 3 armpit sts in reverse st st):

Next row (RS): cast off 3 sts, work to end in pattern.

Next row (WS): work to last 4 sts, k2tog, k2.

Next row (RS): work to end in pattern.

Repeat last 2 rows 8 (9, 9, 10, 10) times more, then work 1 more decrease row. Break yarn and place remaining 4 (5, 7, 8, 10) sts on spare yarn.

Sleeves (make 2)
CO 25 (25, 27, 27, 29) sts.

Next row (WS): *k1, p1, repeat from * to last st, k1.

Next row (RS): *p1, k1, repeat from * to last st, p1.

Repeat last 2 rows once more, then work 1 more WS row.

Work cable pattern as follows:
Row 1: p2 (2, 3, 3, 4), pm, sl 1, k2, p1, k4, p1, k1, p1, k1, p1, k4, p1, k2, sl 1, pm, p to end.

Row 2: k to marker, sl marker, sl 1, p2, k1, p5, k1, p1, k1, p5, k1, p2, sl 1, sl marker, k to end.

Row 3: p to marker, sl marker, C3F, p1, C4B, p1, k1, p1, k1, p1, C4F, p1, C3B, sl marker, p to end.

Row 4: k to marker, sl marker, p3, k1, p5, k1, p1, k1, p5, k1, p3, sl marker, k to end.

Row 1 (increase row): p2, m1p, p to marker, sl marker, sl 1, k2, p1, k4, p1, k1, p1, k1, p1, k4, p1, k2, sl 1, sl marker, p to last 2 sts, m1p, p to end. 27 (27, 29, 29, 31) sts.

Row 2: k to marker, sl marker, sl 1, p2, k1, p5, k1, p1, k1, p5, k1, p2, sl 1, sl marker, k to end.

Row 3: p to marker, sl marker, C3F, p1, C4B, p1, k1, p1, k1, p1, C4F, p1, C3B, sl marker, p to end.

Row 4: k to marker, sl marker, p3, k1, p5, k1, p1, k1, p5, k1, p3, sl marker, k to end.

Row 5: p to marker, sl marker, sl 1, k2, p1, k4, p1, k1, p1, k1, p1, k4, p1, k2, sl 1, sl marker, p to end.

Row 6: as Row 2.

Row 7: as Row 3.

Row 8: as Row 4.

Repeat last 8 rows 4 times more, until you have 35 (35, 37, 37, 39) sts.

Work straight in pattern until piece measures 20cm (21cm, 22cm, 24cm, 26cm) from cast-on edge, ending with a RS row.

Cast off 3 sts at the beginning of the next 2 rows.

Begin working decreases. (**Note:** as your work decreases, you will no longer be able to work the cable sts as written for all the sts. Work those sts in st st, keeping 3 armpit sts in reverse st st.)

Next row (WS): k2, ssk, work to last 4 sts, k2tog, k2.

Next row (RS): work next RS row.

Repeat last 2 rows 8 (9, 9, 10, 10) times more, then work 1 more decrease row. Break yarn and place remaining 9 (7, 9, 7, 9) sts on spare yarn.

Join pieces
Place Right Front sts on needle with RS facing. Attach yarn and work to last 2 (2, 3, 3, 3) sts.

Sizes 12–18 months and 18–24 months only: k2tog.

Sizes 2T, 3T and 4T: sl 1-k2tog-psso.

Place First Sleeve sts on needle with RS facing. Using working yarn attached to Right Front, work as follows:

Sizes 12–18 months and 18–24 months only: ssk, work to last 2 sts, k2tog.

Sizes 2T, 3T and 4T: sl 1-k2tog-psso, work to last 3 sts, sl 1-k2tog-psso.

Place Back sts on needle with RS facing. Using working yarn attached to First Sleeve, work as follows:

Sizes 12–18 months and 18–24 months only: ssk, work to last 2 sts, k2tog.

Sizes 2T, 3T and 4T: sl 1-k2tog-psso, work to last 3 sts, sl 1-k2tog-psso.

Place Second Sleeve sts on needle with RS facing. Using working yarn attached to Back, work as follows:

Sizes 12–18 months and 18–24 months only: ssk, work to last 2 sts, k2tog.

Sizes 2T, 3T and 4T: sl 1-k2tog-psso, work to last 3 sts, sl 1-k2tog-psso.

Place Left Front sts on needle with RS facing. Using working yarn attached to Second Sleeve, work as follows:

Sizes 12–18 months and 18–24 months only: work to last 2 sts, k2tog.

Sizes 2T, 3T and 4T: work to last 3 sts, sl 1-k2tog-psso. 35 (33, 35, 33, 43) sts.

Size 4T only

Next row (WS): work 6, k2tog, work 3, k2tog, work 17, k2tog, work 3, k2tog, work to end. 39 sts.

Sizes 12–18 months, 18–24 months, 2T and 3T only

Next row: work to end in pattern.

All sizes

Next row (RS): *p1, k1, repeat from * to last st, p1.

Next row (WS): *k1, p1, repeat from * to last st, k1.

Next row (RS): *p1, k1, repeat from * to last st, p1.

Next row (WS): *k1, p1, repeat from * to last st, k1.

Cast off all sts in rib pattern.

Finishing

Starting at the top and working your way down, with RS facing, sew together raglan seams, then side seams, then sleeve seams, using mattress stitch (see page 16). Weave in ends.

Button Band

Starting at bottom edge of Right Front, with RS facing, pick up and k 49 (53, 57, 63, 67) sts along side edge.

Next row (WS): *k1, p1, repeat from * to last st, k1.

Repeat this row once more.

Next row (WS): k1, p1, yf, p2tog, [work 8 (9, 10, 11, 12), yf, p2tog] x 4, work to end.

Next row (RS): *k1, p1, repeat from * to last st, k1.

Cast off all sts in moss stitch pattern.

Starting at top edge of Left Front, with RS facing, pick up and k 49 (53, 57, 63, 67) sts along side edge.

Next row (WS): *k1, p1, repeat from * to last st, k1.

Repeat this row 3 times more.

Cast off all sts in moss stitch pattern.

Weave in ends.

To block, soak in lukewarm water for a few minutes, then lay flat to dry, taking care to press the reverse st st seams so they lay flat. Sew buttons opposite buttonholes.

Avery Pullover

This is a stylish and classy pullover – much like Maile's school friend, Avery. The six-stitch cable at the raglan shaping is very simple to work and it branches out into a twelve-stitch looping cable at the sides, giving the sweater a subtle touch of something special.

Sizes

12–18 months (18–24 months, 2T, 3T, 4T) (shown in 2T)

Materials

- 1 (1, 2, 2, 2) x 115g skeins SweetGeorgia Superwash DK (shade: Mist)
- 1 x 4mm 40cm circular needle
- 1 x set of 4mm double-pointed needles
- 9 x stitch markers
- Cable needle
- Tapestry needle
- Spare yarn

Tension

21.5 sts and 28 rows to 10cm over st st using 4mm needles.

Cable patterns

6-stitch cable right

Row 1: k to end.
Row 2: k to end.
Row 3: C6B.
Row 4: k to end.

6-stitch cable left

Row 1: k to end.
Row 2: k to end.
Row 3: C6F.
Row 4: k to end.

12-stitch cable right

Rows 1–9: k3, p6, k3.
Row 10: T6F, T6B.
Row 11: p3, k6, p3.
Row 12: p3, C6F, p3.
Row 13: p3, k6, p3.
Row 14: T6B, T6F.

12-stitch cable left

Rows 1–9: k3, p6, k3.
Row 10: T6F, T6B.
Row 11: p3, k6, p3.
Row 12: p3, C6B, p3.
Row 13: p3, k6, p3.
Row 14: T6B, T6F.

Pattern

Yoke

CO 66 (72, 78, 84, 90) sts using circular needle, pm and join to work in the round.

Next round: *k3, p3, repeat from * to end. Repeat last round 4 times more.

Set-up round: k7 (8, 9, 10, 11), p1, pm, work Row 1 of 6-stitch cable right, pm, p1, k2 (3, 4, 5, 6), p1, pm, work Row 1 of 6-stitch cable left, pm, p1, k15 (17, 19, 21, 23), p1, pm, work Row 1 of 6-stitch cable right, pm, p1, k2 (3, 4, 5, 6), p1, pm, work Row 1 of 6-stitch cable left, pm, p1, k to end.

***Raglan round:** [k to 1 st before marker, m1, p1, sl marker, work Row 2 of 6-stitch cable right, sl marker, p1, m1, k to 1 st before marker, m1, p1, sl marker, work Row 2 of 6-stitch cable left, sl marker, p1, m1] x 2, k to end.

Next round: [k to 1 st before marker, p1, sl marker, work Row 3 of 6-stitch cable right, sl marker, p1, k to 1 st before marker, p1, sl marker, Row 3 of 6-stitch cable left, sl marker, p1] x 2, k to end.

Repeat from * 11 (11, 11, 12, 12) times more until you have 162 (168, 174, 188, 194) sts, working next row of 6-stitch cable as you go.

Divide for sleeves

Next round: [k to 1 st before marker, p1, sl marker, k3, sl next 3 sts onto spare yarn, remove marker, sl next 28 (29, 30, 33, 34) sts on spare yarn, remove marker, sl next 3 sts onto spare yarn, CO 6 sts, k3, sl marker, p1] x 2, k to end of round. 106 (110, 118, 122, 126) sts on needles.

Body

Set-up round: k to 1 st before marker, p1, sl marker, work Row 1 of 12-stitch cable right, sl marker, p1, k to 1 st before marker, p1, sl marker, work Row 1 of 12-stitch cable left, sl marker, p1, k to end.

****Next round:** k to 1 st before marker, p1, sl marker, work Row 2 of 12-stitch cable right, sl marker, p1, k to 1 st before marker, p1, sl marker, work Row 2 of 12-stitch cable left, sl marker, p1, k to end.

Repeat previous round 8 (10, 12, 14, 16) times more, working next row of 12-stitch cable right and 12-stitch cable left as you go.

Increase round: k to 2 sts before marker, m1, k1, p1, sl marker, work next row of 12-stitch cable right, sl marker, p1, k1, m1, k to 2 sts before marker, m1, k1, p1, sl marker, work next row of 12-stitch cable left, sl marker, p1, k1, m1, k to end. 110 (114, 122, 126, 130) sts.

Repeat from ** twice more. 118 (122, 130, 134, 138) sts.

Work straight in pattern until piece measures 29cm (30cm, 31cm, 33cm, 34cm) from cast-on edge.

Sizes 12–18 months and 2T only

Next round: k59 (65), m1, k to last st, m1, k1. 120 (132) sts.

Sizes 18–24 months and 3T only

Next round: k1, m1, k58 (65), m1, k2, m1, k to last st, m1, k1. 126 (138) sts.

All sizes

Next round: *k3, p3, repeat from * to end. Repeat last round 4 times more. Cast off all sts in pattern.

Sleeves

With WS facing, place left sleeve sts on dpns and attach yarn, p to end of row, then pick up 3 sts from cast-on edge at point at which work was divided for sleeves.

Next row (RS): k to end, then pick up 3 sts from cast-on edge under arm, pm and, with RS facing, join to work in the round. 40 (41, 42, 45, 46) sts.

***K 8 (10, 12, 14, 16) rounds.

Next round: k2, ssk, k to last 4 sts, k2tog, k2.
38 (39, 40, 43, 44) sts. Repeat from *** twice more.
34 (35, 36, 39, 40) sts.

Work straight in pattern until sleeve measures 19.5cm
(20.5cm, 21cm, 23cm, 25cm).

Sizes 12–18 months, 18–24 months and 3T only
Next round: Decrease 4 (5, 1) st(s) spaced 8 (8, 30) sts
apart, k to end. 30 (30, 36) sts.

All sizes
Next row: *k3, p3, repeat from * to end. Repeat last
round 4 times more. Cast off all stitches in pattern. Repeat
with second sleeve.

Finishing
Weave in ends. Using ends of yarn at underarm, stitch closed
the gaps around the picked up stitches. Block lightly, taking
care not to squish or stretch out the cables at the sides.

Chevron Hat

This colourful hat is a fun and comfortable twist on a striped beanie. The pretty chevron pattern is tightly woven, keeping the hat snugly in place.

Sizes

12–24 months (2T–3T, 4T) (shown in 2T–3T)

Materials

- 1 x 50g ball Debbie Bliss Cotton DK (shade: 13019 Stone) for MC
- 1 x 50g ball Debbie Bliss Cotton DK (shade: 13018 Navy) for CC1
- 1 x 50g ball Debbie Bliss Cotton DK (shade: 13052 Mink) for CC2
- 1 x 50g ball Debbie Bliss Cotton DK (shade: 13064 Coral) for CC3
- 1 x 50g ball Debbie Bliss Cotton DK (shade: 13061 Aqua) for CC4
- 1 x 3.75mm 30cm circular needles
- 1 x set of 3.75mm double-pointed needles
- Tapestry needle

Tension

22 sts and 30 rows to 10cm st st using 3.75mm needles.

Pattern

Using MC and circular needle, CO 84 (92, 100) sts, pm and join to work in the round.
Next round: *k2, p2, repeat from * to end. Repeat this round for 3cm (3.5cm, 4cm).

Next round: *k3, m1, k2, m1, repeat from * to last 14

(2, 0) sts. **Sizes 12–24 months and 2T–3T only:** [k2 (1), m1] x 6 (2), k to end. 120 (130, 140) sts.

Round 1: *sl 1, m1, k3, sl 1-k2tog-psso, k3, m1, repeat from * to end.

Round 2: *k1tbl, k9, repeat from * to end.

Work Rounds 1 and 2 2 (2, 3) times more.

*Change to CC1. Work Rounds 1 & 2 twice more.

Change to CC2. Work Rounds 1 and 2 2 (3, 3) times.
Change to CC3. Work Rounds 1 and 2 once more.
Change to CC4. Work Rounds 1 and 2 2 (2, 3) times.

Repeat from * once more. Change to MC. Work Rounds 1 and 2 2 (2, 3) times.

Round 3: *sl 1, k3, sl 1-k2tog-psso, k3, repeat from * to end. 96 (104, 112) sts.

Round 4: *k1tbl, k7, repeat from * to end.

Round 5: *sl 1, k2, sl 1-k2tog-psso, k2, repeat from * to end. 72 (78, 84) sts.

Round 6: *k1tbl, k5, repeat from * to end.

Round 7: *sl 1, k1, sl 1-k2tog-psso, k1, repeat from * to end. 48 (52, 56) sts.

Round 8: *k1tbl, k3, repeat from * to end.

Round 9: *sl 1, sl 1-k2tog-psso, repeat from * to end.
24 (26, 28) sts.

Round 10: *k1tbl, k1, repeat from * to end.

Round 11: *sl 1-k2tog-psso, repeat from * to last 2 sts,
skp. 8 (9, 10) sts.

Break yarn, leaving a long tail. Draw tail through remaining
sts and pull tight, closing the hole.

Finishing
Weave in ends. Dunk hat in lukewarm water and swish it
around to relax the stitches. Lay flat to dry, stretching the
hat lengthways a bit.

101

Dandelion Sweater

In a city filled with gardens, dandelions are the only flowers Maile is allowed to pick – and pick them she does. Believe me, when your daughter brings you a bouquet, whatever flower she uses will quickly become your favourite.

Sizes

12–18 months (18–24 months, 2T, 3T and 4T) (shown in 3T)

Materials

- 2 (2, 3, 3, 4) x 50g balls Debbie Bliss Rialto 4-ply (shade: 12 Pale Blue) for MC
- 1 x 50g ball Debbie Bliss Rialto 4-ply (shade: 28 Tangerine) for CC1
- 1 x 50g ball Debbie Bliss Rialto 4-ply (shade: 32 Leaf) for CC2
- 1 x 50g ball Debbie Bliss Rialto 4-ply (shade: 39 Amber) for CC3
- 1 x 3.5mm 40cm circular needle
- 1 x set of 3.5mm double-pointed needles
- 3 stitch markers
- Spare yarn
- Tapestry needle

Tension

28 sts and 39 rows to 10cm over st st using 3.5mm needles.

Roses pattern

Round 1: *k1 CC1, k1 MC, repeat from * to end.

Round 2: *k1 MC, k1 CC1, k1 MC, k1 CC2, repeat from * to end.

Round 3: as Round 1.

Pattern

Body

Using MC and circular needle, CO 136 (144, 152, 160, 168) sts, pm and join to work in the round.

Round 1: *k1, p1, repeat from * to end. Repeat last round until piece measures 3cm from cast-on edge.

K 3 rounds.

Attach CC1 and CC2 and work Rounds 1–3 of Roses pattern once. Break CC1 and CC2.

Using MC, work evenly in st st until piece measures 18cm (19cm, 20cm, 22cm, 23cm) from hem.

Next round: k28 (30, 30, 32, 33), break yarn, place next 12 (12, 16, 16, 18) sts on spare yarn. Reattach yarn, k56 (60, 60, 64, 66), break yarn, place next 12 (12, 16, 16, 18) sts on spare yarn. Reattach yarn, k to end of round. Set aside, leaving working yarn attached.

Sleeves (make 2)

Using dpns and a new ball of MC, CO 40 (44, 48, 52, 56) sts, pm and join to work in the round.

Next round: *k1, p1, repeat from * to end. Repeat last round until piece measures 3cm from cast-on edge.

K 3 rounds.

Attach CC1 and CC2 and work Rounds 1–3 of Roses pattern once. Break CC1 and CC2.

Using MC, k 2 rounds.

Next round: k1, m1, k to last st, m1, k1. 42 (46, 50, 54, 58) sts.

*K 4 (4, 6, 6, 8) rounds.

Next round: k1, m1, k to last st, m1, k1. 44 (48, 52, 56, 60) sts.

Repeat from * 4 times more. 52 (56, 60, 64, 68) sts.

Work straight until sleeve measures 21cm (22cm, 23cm, 25cm, 27cm) from bottom of cuff.

Next round: k to last 6 (6, 8, 8, 9) sts, place next 12 (12, 16, 16, 18) sts on spare yarn. Break yarn and set aside.

Yoke

Join Body and Sleeves

Return to body piece.

Next round: using the circular needle, k28 (30, 30, 32, 33) sts to sleeve break of body, k across 40 (44, 44, 48, 50) sts of 1st sleeve, k across 56 (60, 60, 64, 66) sts of front of body, k across 40 (44, 44, 48, 50) sts of 2nd sleeve, k 28 (30, 30, 32, 33) sts to end-of-round marker on body. 192 (208, 208, 224, 232) sts.

K 2 (2, 4, 4, 6) rounds.

Attach CC1 and CC2 and work Rounds 1–3 of Roses pattern once. Break CC1. Do not break CC2.

K 1 (1, 2, 2, 3) round(s).

Next round: *k1, k2tog, repeat from * to last 0 (1, 1, 2, 1) st(s), k to end. 128 (139, 139, 150, 155) sts.

Size 12–18 months only
Next round: *k14, k2tog, repeat from * to end. 120 sts.

Sizes 18–24 months and 2T only
Next round: *k17, k2tog, repeat from * to last 6 sts, k to end. 132 sts.

Size 3T only
Next round: *k23, k2tog, repeat from * to end. 144 sts.

Size 4T only
Next round: k3, m1, k to end. 156 sts.

All sizes
K 1 (1, 2, 2, 3) round(s).

Work Dandelions pattern once as follows:
Round 1: k CC2.

Round 2: k CC2.

Round 3: k1 MC, k1 CC2, *k2 MC, k1 CC2, repeat from * to last st, k1 MC.

Round 4: k4 MC, k1 CC2, *k11 MC, k1 CC2, repeat from * to last 7 sts, k to end MC.

Round 5: as Round 4.

Round 6: as Round 4.

Round 7: as Round 4.

Round 8: k4 MC, k1 CC3, *k11 MC, k1 CC3, repeat from * to last 7 sts, k to end MC.

Round 9: k3 MC, k3 CC3, k8 MC, k1 CC3, k1 MC, k1 CC3, k1 MC, k1 CC3, *k8 MC, k3 CC3, k8 MC, k1 CC3, k1 MC, k1 CC3, k1 MC, k1 CC3, repeat from * to last 5 (17, 17, 5, 17) sts.
Sizes 12–18 months and 3T only: k to end MC.
Sizes 18–24 months (2T, 4T) only: k8 MC, k3 CC3, k to end MC.

Round 10: k2 MC, k5 CC3, k8 MC, k3 CC3, *k8 MC, k5 CC3, k8 MC, k3 CC3, repeat from * to last 6 (18, 18, 6, 18) sts.
Sizes 12–18 months and 3T only: k to end MC.
Sizes 18–24 months (2T, 4T) only: k8 MC, k3 CC3, k to end MC.

Round 11: k1 MC, k7 CC3, *k5 MC, k7 CC3, repeat from * to last 4 sts, k to end MC.

Round 12: k9 CC3, k6 MC, k3 CC3, *k6 MC, k9 CC3, k6 MC, k3 CC3, repeat from * to last 6 (18, 18, 6, 18) sts.
Sizes 12–18 months and 3T only: k to end MC.
Sizes 18–24 months (2T, 4T) only: k6 MC, k9 CC3, k to end MC.

Round 13: k2 MC, k5 CC3, k7 MC, k1 CC3, k1 MC, k1 CC3, k1 MC, k1 CC3, *k7 MC, k5 CC3, k7 MC, k1 CC3, k1 MC, k1 CC3, k1 MC, k1 CC3, repeat from * to last 5 (17, 17, 5, 17) sts.
Sizes 12–18 months and 3T only: k to end MC.
Sizes 18–24 months (2T, 4T) only: k7 MC, k5 CC3, k to end MC.
Round 14: k3 MC, k3 CC3, k10 MC, k1 CC3, *k10 MC, k3 CC3, k10 MC, k1 CC3, repeat from * to last 7 (19, 19, 7, 19) sts.

Sizes 12–18 months and 3T only: k to end MC.
Sizes 18–24 months (2T, 4T) only: k7 MC, k3 CC3, k to end MC. Break CC3.

Next round: using MC, k to end.

Next round: *k2, k2tog, repeat from * to end. 90 (99, 99, 108, 117) sts.

Size 12–18 months only
Next round: *k43, k2tog, repeat from * to end. 88 sts.

Sizes 18–24 months and 2T only
Next round: *k31, k2tog, repeat from * to end. 96 sts.

Size 3T only
Next round: k to end. 108 sts.

Size 4T only
Next round: k1, k2tog, k to end. 116 sts.

All sizes
Attach CC1 and work Rounds 1–3 of Roses pattern once. Break CC1 and CC2.

Next round: using MC, k to end.

Next round: *k3, k2tog, repeat from * to last 3 (1, 1, 3, 1) st(s), k to end. 71 (77, 77, 87, 93) sts.

Next round: k1, k2tog, k to end. 70 (76, 76, 86, 92) sts.

Next round: *k1, p1, repeat from * to end. Repeat last round until ribbing measures 2cm. Cast off all sts in pattern.

Finishing
Place held underarm stitches on needles and graft top and bottom held underarm stitches together using Kitchener stitch (see page 17). Weave in ends. To block, soak in lukewarm water for at least 5 minutes to relax the stitches, then stretch flat to dry.

Chapter 3

Toys & Miscellany

Octopus

What did the Little Octopus say to the Mama Octopus? 'Can I hold your hand hand hand hand hand hand hand hand?'

Size

One size

Materials

- 1 x 100g skein Manos Maxima (shade: 2342 Eucalyptus)
- 1 x set of 4mm double-pointed needles
- 9 x stitch markers
- Tapestry needle
- Safety pin
- Stuffing
- Black and white felt pieces
- Needle and thread

Tension

20 sts and 28.5 rows to 10cm over st st using 4mm needles

Pattern

Head

CO 28 sts using the provisional cast-on method (see page 12), pm and join to work in the round.

Next round: k3, *pm, k1, pm, k6, repeat from * to last 4 sts, pm, k1, pm, k3.

K 3 rounds.

Next round: *[k to marker, m1, sl marker, k1, sl marker, m1] x 4, k to end. 36 sts.

K 4 rounds.

Repeat from * 5 times more. 76 sts.

**K 4 rounds.

Next round: [k to 2 sts before marker, ssk, sl marker, k1, sl marker, k2tog] x 4, k to end. 68 sts. Repeat from ** twice more. 52 sts. ***K 2 rounds.

Next round: [k to 2 sts before marker, ssk, sl marker, k1, sl marker, k2tog] x 4, k to end. 44 sts. Repeat from *** twice more. 28 sts.

Next round: k to end.

Next round: [k to 2 sts before marker, ssk, sl marker, k1, sl marker, k2tog] x 4, k to end. 20 sts.

Next round: k to end, removing markers.

Next round: *k2tog, repeat from * to end. 10 sts.

Break yarn, leaving a long tail. Draw yarn through remaining sts and pull tight.

Finishing

Weave in ends. Sew felt eyes and mouth on Head as pictured. Stuff Head. Place a safety pin to mark the cast-on row. Unravel provisional cast-on and place 28 sts on dpns. Join to work in the round.

Next round: k to end.

Next round: *k2tog, repeat from * to end. 14 sts.

K 2 rounds.

Next round: *k2tog, repeat from * to end. 7 sts.

Break yarn, leaving a long tail. Draw tail through remaining sts and pull tight, closing Head. Weave in end.

Arms

Insert tip of dpn into a st 3 rows above the cast-on round. Continue to insert tip along this round, until you have picked up 8 sts. Using a 2nd dpn, insert tip into 8 sts along the round just above this one, so they are held parallel. Using a 3rd dpn, k picked up sts from the bottom needle, then the top needle, working in the round. K for 12cm.

Stuff lightly – you don't want the arm to stick out too far. As you work the following rounds, continue to stuff the arm as you go – you won't need much stuffing, but you don't want the tip of the arm to be floppy.

Next round: k3 sts from top dpn, k2tog, k to end of round. 15 sts.

K 4 rounds.

Next round: k2, sl 1-k2tog-psso, k to end of round. 13 sts.

K 4 rounds.

Next round: k1, sl 1-k2tog-psso, k to end of round. 11 sts.

K 4 rounds.

Next round: sl 1-k2tog-psso, k to end of round. 9 sts.

Top dpn has 1 st, and bottom dpn has 8 sts. Sl 2 sts from each end of bottom dpn onto top dpn. Top dpn now has 5 sts, bottom dpn has 4 sts.

Next round: k to end.

Next round: k1, sl 1-k2tog-psso, k1, k to end. 7 sts.

Next round: k to end.

Next round: sl 1-k2tog-psso, k to end. 5 sts.

Break yarn, leaving a long tail. Pull tail through remaining 5 sts and pull tight, closing Arm. Weave in ends.

Note: If picking up stitches and working the yarn from the body feels too tight or too tricky, you can certainly work the arms separately and sew them on afterwards. Just be sure not to overstuff the bottoms of the arms; sew the opening of each arm so that it's nearly closed, so that the arms remain floppy.

Work 3 more Arms around the base of the head, as above. Don't worry if they aren't perfectly evenly spaced, or if you don't manage to line them up on the exact same round – the arms can be slightly uneven and still look fine.

Choose a round on the Head 4 rounds above the one you've been working along. Place 4 more Arms around this round, between the 4 lower Arms as pictured.

All finished!

Blocks

Maile loves carefully placing these stackable blocks on top of each other, then knocking them down like Godzilla. The magic loop technique, if you're familiar with it, is good for this pattern if you have a long circular needle, but double-pointed needles will do just as well.

Sizes

Block 1: 16 x 16cm, Block 2: 13 x 13cm,
Block 3: 11 x 11cm, Block 4: 8.5 x 8.5cm

Materials

- 2 x 100g balls Rowan Creative Focus Worsted (shade: 1265 New Fern) for MC
- 1 x 100g ball Rowan Creative Focus Worsted (shade: 3089 Blue Smoke) for CC1
- 1 x 100g ball Rowan Creative Focus Worsted (shade: 0410 Espresso) for CC2
- 1 x 100g ball Rowan Creative Focus Worsted (shade: 1107 Cobalt) for CC3
- 1 x set of 4.5mm double-pointed needles
- 1 x 4.5mm 40cm circular needle
- 9 x stitch markers
- Tapestry needle
- Embroidery needle
- Thread
- Polyester stuffing

Tension

20 sts and 24 rows to 10cm over st st using 4.5mm needles.

Pattern

Block 1

Using MC and dpns, CO 4 sts.
Next row: kf&b in every st. 8 sts.
Place end-of-round marker and join to work in the round.

Next round: p to end.

Next round: kf&b in every st. 16 sts.

Next round: p1, pm, p1, pm, p3, pm, p1, pm, p3, pm, p1, pm, p3, pm, p1, pm, p2.

Next round: *[k to marker, m1, sl marker, k1, sl marker, m1] x 4, k to end.

Next round: p to end.
Repeat from * 3 times more. 48 sts.

Next round: **[k to marker, m1, sl marker, k1, sl marker, m1] x 4, k to end. 56 sts.

Next round: k to end.
Repeat from ** 4 times more, changing to the circular needle when you have enough sts to do so. 88 sts.

Next round: ***[k to marker, m1, sl marker, k1, sl marker, m1] x 4, k to end.

Next round: p to end.
Repeat from *** 4 times more. 128 sts.

Next round: [k to marker, m1, sl marker, k1, sl marker, m1] x 4, k to end. 136 sts. Cast off all sts purlwise.

Work 3 more blocks in MC and 2 blocks in CC3.

Block 2
Using CC1 and dpns, CO 4 sts.
Next row: kf&b in every st. 8 sts.
Place end-of-round marker and join to work in the round.

Next round: p to end.

Next round: kf&b in every st. 16 sts.

Next round: p1, pm, p1, pm, p3, pm, p1, pm, p3, pm, p1, pm, p3, pm, p1, pm, p2.

Next round: *[k to marker, m1, sl marker, k1, sl marker, m1] x 4, k to end. 24 sts.

Next round: p to end.
Repeat from * twice more. 40 sts.

Next round: **[k to marker, m1, sl marker, k1, sl marker, m1] x 4, k to end. 48 sts.

Next round: k to end.
Repeat from ** 3 times more, changing to circular needle when you have enough sts to do so. 72 sts.

Next round: ***[k to marker, m1, sl marker, k1, sl marker, m1] x 4, k to end. 80 sts.

Next round: p to end.
Repeat from *** 3 times more. 104 sts.

Next round: [k to marker, m1, sl marker, k1, sl marker, m1] x 4, k to end. 112 sts.
Cast off all sts purlwise.

Work 3 more blocks in CC1 and 2 blocks in CC2.

Block 3
Using CC3 and dpns, CO 4 sts.
Next row: kf&b in every st. 8 sts.
Place end-of-round marker and join to work in the round.

Next round: p to end.

Next round: kf&b in every st. 16 sts.

Next round: p1, pm, p1, pm, p3, pm, p1, pm, p3, pm, p1, pm, p3, pm, p1, pm, p2.

Next round: *[k to marker, m1, sl marker, k1, sl marker, m1] x 4, k to end. 24 sts.

Next round: p to end.
Repeat from * once more. 32 sts.

Next round: **[k to marker, m1, sl marker, k1, sl marker, m1] x 4, k to end. 40 sts.

Next round: k to end.
Repeat from ** twice more. 56 sts.

Next round: ***[k to marker, m1, sl marker, k1, sl marker, m1] x 4, k to end. 64 sts.

Next round: p to end.
Repeat from *** twice more, changing to circular needle when you have enough sts to do so. 80 sts.

Next round: [k to marker, m1, sl marker, k1, sl marker, m1] x 4, k to end. 88 sts. Cast off all sts purlwise.

Work 3 more blocks in CC3 and 2 blocks in CC1.

Block 4
Using CC2 and dpns, CO 4 sts.
Next row: kf&b in every st. 8 sts.
Place end-of-round marker and join to work in the round.

Next round: p to end.

Next round: kf&b in every st. 16 sts.

Next round: p1, pm, p1, pm, p3, pm, p1, pm, p3, pm, p1, pm, p3, pm, p1, pm, p2.

Next round: [k to marker, m1, sl marker, k1, sl marker, m1] x 4, k to end. 24 sts.

Next round: p to end.

Next round: *[k to marker, m1, sl marker, k1, sl marker, m1] x 4, k to end. 32 sts.

Next round: k to end.
Repeat from * once. 40 sts.

Next round: **[k to marker, m1, sl marker, k1, sl marker, m1] x 4, k to end. 48 sts.

Next round: p to end.
Repeat from ** once. 56 sts.

Next round: [k to marker, m1, sl marker, k1, sl marker, m1] x 4, k to end. Cast off all sts purlwise.

Work 3 more blocks in CC2 and 2 blocks in MC.

Finishing

Felt by tossing the blocks into the washing machine with a pair of old jeans. Run a cycle with a warm setting that is fairly gentle and check it often. You want the pieces to felt just enough to make the fabric slightly stiffened and the stitches a bit blurred. The pieces should not shrink much. Sew the blocks together using mattress stitch (see page 18) and the contrast colour (i.e. the colour used on only two sides of the block). Leave one side of the final square unsewn, and stuff with polyester stuffing. Sew closed and weave in ends.

Duckling Puppet

This charming little character is sized for all hands, big and small. He's so cute it's hard to resist picking him up and playing with him, and he's so endearing that he's bound to hang around a while – perhaps as an heirloom piece when your little one gets too grown up for him but likes to remember his lively yellow-and-orange friend.

Size

One size

Materials

- 1 x 100g skein Malabrigo Merino Worsted (shade: 19 Pollen) for MC
- 1x 100g skein Malabrigo Merino Worsted (shade: 16 Glazed Carrot) for CC (note: only a very small amount of this skein is used)
- 1 x set of 4.5mm double-pointed needles
- Tapestry needle
- Needle and thread
- 2 x 13mm buttons (or, for younger recipients, sew on felt eyes instead)

Tension

20 sts and 29.5 rows to 10cm over st st using 4.5mm needles.

Pattern

Body

Using MC, CO 50 sts, pm and join to work in the round.

Next round: p to end.

Next round: k to end.

Next round: p to end.

Next round: k to end.

Next round: p to end.

Work straight in k until you have 8cm of st st.

Create beak and wing openings

Next round: k11, cast off 3 sts, k22, cast off 3 sts, k to end.

Next round: k to cast-off edge and turn. Begin working in rows; work to opposite cast-off edge, leaving 22 Front sts on a dpn or a st holder. Work 10 rows in st st.

Break yarn and set needle aside (or place on a st holder). Attach yarn at held 22 Front sts with RS facing.

K 12 rows, ending with a WS row.

Next row: K 1 row, CO 3 sts using backward-loop cast-on method (see page 13), k across 1st 11 held sts, sl marker, k11, CO 3 sts using backward-loop cast-on method. Join to work in the round and k to marker.

Using marker as the end of round, k 3 rounds.

Next row: k18, cast off 14 sts. Leaving marker in place, k to cast-off edge. Turn to begin working in rows and work 2 rows in st st, ending with a RS row.

Next row: CO 14 sts, divide sts among dpns, join to work in the round and k to marker.

Shape head

Using marker as the end of round, work in st st for 4cm.
Next round: *k8, k2tog, repeat from * to end. 45 sts.

Next round: k to end.

Next round: *k7, k2tog, repeat from * to end. 40 sts.

Next round: k to end.

Next round: *k6, k2tog, repeat from * to end. 35 sts.

Next round: k to end.

Next round: *k5, k2tog, repeat from * to end. 30 sts.

Next round: k to end.

Next round: *k4, k2tog, repeat from * to end. 25 sts.

Next round: *k3, k2tog, repeat from * to end. 20 sts.

Next round: *2, k2tog, repeat from * to end. 15 sts.

Next round: *k1, k2tog, repeat from * to end. 10 sts.

Break yarn, leaving a long tail. Draw tail through remaining sts and pull tight, closing the hole.

Wings

Beginning at centre bottom of left wing opening, pick up and k 30 sts. Divide evenly among dpns, pm and join to work in the round.

Work in k until wing measures 3cm from cast-on edge.

Next round: *k1, ssk, k to last 3 sts, k2tog, k1. 28 sts.

K for 2 rounds.

Repeat from * twice more. 24 sts.

Next round: **k1, ssk, k to last 3 sts, k2tog, k1. 22 sts.

Next round: k to end.
Repeat from ** once more. 20 sts.

***K1, ssk, k to last 3 sts, k2tog, k1.
Repeat from *** 6 times more.

Next round: k1, ssk, k2tog, k1. 4 sts.

Break yarn, leaving a long tail. Draw tail through remaining sts and pull tight, closing the hole.

Work right wing as for left wing, beginning at the centre bottom of the right wing opening.

Beak

Beginning at bottom left corner of beak opening, using CC, pick up and k 20 sts across bottom edge.

Next row: p to end.

Next row: k to end.

CO 16 sts using backward loop cast-on method, divide sts evenly across needles, pm and join to work in the round.

Next round: k to end.

Next round: k1, ssk, k14, k2tog, k2, ssk, k10, k2tog, k1.
32 sts.

Next round: k to end.

Next round: k1, ssk, k12, k2tog, k2, ssk, k8, k2tog, k1.
28 sts.

Next round: k to end.

Next round: k1, ssk, k10, k2tog, k2, ssk, k6, k2tog, k1.
24 sts.

Next round: k to end.

Next round: k1, ssk, k8, k2tog, k2, ssk, k4, k2tog, k1.
20 sts.

Next round: k to end.

Next round: k1, ssk, k6, k2tog, k2, ssk, k2, k2tog, k1.
16 sts.

Next round: k to end.

Next round: k1, ssk, k4, k2tog, k2, ssk, k2tog, k1. 12 sts.

Next round: k to end.

Next round: k1, ssk, k2, k2tog, k1, ssk, k2tog. 8 sts.

Next round: k to end.

Next round: k1, ssk, k2tog, k1, k2tog. 5 sts.

Break yarn, leaving a long tail. Draw tail through remaining
sts and pull tight, closing the hole.

Beginning at top right corner of beak opening, using CC,
pick up and k 20 sts across top edge.

Work as for bottom beak.

Finishing

Weave in ends. Sew edges of beak together. Sew on
button eyes as pictured.

To make a pom-pom, cut a rectangular piece of cardboard
about 3cm wide and 4cm long. Wind both MC and CC
around the cardboard many, many times – the more times
you wind, the puffier your pom-pom will be. Break yarn.
Using MC, insert your tapestry needle under your windings
against the cardboard. Cinch a very tight knot around the
windings and ensure it will hold. Break yarn, leaving a
long tail. Turn the cardboard over and snip the yarn on the
opposite side from where you've tied your knot. Then trim
your pom-pom to make it evenly round and sized to your
preference. Sew the pom-pom on top of the puppet using
the long tail.

Magpie Pouch

Like magpies, children often like to collect shiny little things, or rocks, or shells. This bag is meant for those special treasures.

Size

One size

Materials

- 1 x 50g ball S. Charles Collezione Adele (shade: 23 Jade)
- 1 x set of 3.75mm double-pointed needles
- 1 x 3.75mm 30cm circular needle
- Stitch marker
- Cable needle
- Tapestry needle
- 40cm of 5mm ribbon

Tension

22 sts and 22 rows to 10cm over st st using 3.75mm needles.

Pattern

Using dpns, cast on 4 sts, pm and join to work in the round.

Next round: kf&b in every st.

Next round: k to end.

Repeat last 2 rounds until you have 128 sts, changing to circular needles when it feels comfortable to do so.

Next round: [k9, kf&b] x 12, k to end. 140 sts.

K 3 rounds.

Round 1: sl 1, k12, *sl 2, k12, repeat from * to last st, sl 1.

Round 2: as Round 1.

Round 3: C3F, *k8, C3B, C3F, repeat from * to last 11 sts, k8, C3B.

Rounds 4–6: k to end.

Round 7: k6, *sl 2, k12, repeat from * to last 8 sts, sl 2, k6.

Round 8: as Round 7.

Round 9: k4, *C3B, C3F, k8, repeat from * to last 10 sts, C3B, C3F, k4.

Round 10: k to end.

Next round: *k8, k2tog, repeat from * to end. 126 sts.

Next round: k to end.

Work Rounds 1–10 once more.

Next round: *k7, k2tog, repeat from * to end. 112 sts.

Next round: k to end.

Work Rounds 1–10 once more.

Next round: *k6, k2tog, repeat from * to end. 98 sts.

Next round: k to end.

Work Rounds 1–10 once more.

Next round: *k5, k2tog, repeat from * to end. 84 sts. (Change to dpns if necessary.)

Next round: k to end.

Work Rounds 1–10 once more.

Next round: *k4, yf, k2tog, repeat from * to end. (Stitch count unchanged.)

Next round: k to end.

Work Rounds 1–10 once more.

Next round: k to end.

Cast off all sts.

Finishing

Weave in ends. Thread tapestry needle with ribbon and weave ribbon into yf holes. Draw tight.

A special bag for rocks, shells, feathers, dried leaves and beach treasures...

Rippling River Scarf & Earwarmer

While I have attempted to keep the suggested yarns machine-washable and child-friendly, I will admit that this yarn, with its nubs of silky colour, is not. But it's so beautiful, and so soft, and knit in a loose cable pattern to imitate the ripples a river makes as it winds its way around the rocks. So it might get drooled on a bit. Toddlers deserve beauty as much as anybody else.

Size

One size

Materials

For Scarf
- 2 x 50g skeins Acadia by The Fibre Company (shade: Oyster)
- 1 x pair of 4mm knitting needles

For Earwarmer
- 1 x 50g skein Acadia by The Fibre Company (shade: Dusk)
- 1 x 4mm 30cm circular needle

For both
- Cable needle

Tension

21 sts and 29 rows to 10cm over st st using 4mm needles.

Scarf Pattern

Using knitting needles, CO 42 sts. K 5 rows.

**Next row (RS): k to end.

Next row (WS): k3, p to last 3 sts, k3.

Next row (RS): k6, C6B, *k3, C6B, repeat from * to last 3 sts, k3.

Next row (WS): k3, p to last 3 sts, k3.

Next row (RS): k to end.

Next row (WS): k3, p to last 3 sts, k3.

Next row (RS): k to end.

Next row (WS): k3, p to last 3 sts, k3.

Next row (RS): k3, *C6F, k3, repeat from * to end.

Next row (WS): k3, p to last 3 sts, k3.

Next row (RS): k to end.

Next row (WS): k3, p to last 3 sts, k3.

Repeat from ** until scarf measures 108cm, ending with a cable row.

Next row: p to end.

K 5 rows. Cast off all sts knitwise.

Earwarmer Pattern

Using circular needle, CO 99 sts. Join to work in the round.

Next round: p to end.

Next round: k to end.

Next round: p to end.

Next round: k to end.

Next round: p to end.

K 2 rounds.

***Cable round 1:** *k3, C6B, repeat from * to end of round.

K 5 rounds.

Cable round 2: *C6F, k3, repeat from * to end of round.

K 5 rounds. Repeat from *** until earwarmer measures 11cm, ending with a cable round.

K 2 rounds.

Next round: p to end.

Next round: k to end.

Next round: p to end.

Next round: k to end. Cast off all sts purlwise.

Buggy Blanket

Despite collecting quite a few blankets when Maile was a baby, I found I needed one more as she grew, something simple and quick to make, that's small, but very warm, and that can be stashed in the buggy or the car for those times when Maile falls asleep on the go.

Size

One size (66 x 61cm)

Materials

- 4 x 100g skeins Spud & Chloë Outer (shade: 7212 Sandbox)
- 1 x 10mm 60cm circular needle
- Tapestry needle

Tension

8.75 sts and 12.5 rows to 10cm over st st using 10mm needles.

Pattern

CO 51 sts.

K 4 rows.

**Starting with a k row, work 6 rows in st st.

Next row (RS): *k1, p1, repeat from * to last st, k1.

Next row: *p1, k1, repeat from * to last st, p1.

Work last 2 rows twice more.

Repeat from ** 4 times more.

Work 6 rows in st st.

P 4 rows.

Cast off all sts purlwise.

***With RS facing, pick up and k 50 sts along right side.

K 4 rows.

Cast off all sts purlwise.

Repeat from *** on left side.

Weave in ends. Block to size.

Ladybird Pillow

For hugging, sleeping on, snuggling and for ladybird picnics – this charming pillow is the ultimate toddler accessory.

Size

One size

Materials

- 2 x 50g balls Debbie Bliss Rialto DK (shade: 03 Black) for MC
- 1 x 50g ball Debbie Bliss Rialto DK (shade: 12 Scarlet) for CC1
- 1 x 50g ball Debbie Bliss Rialto DK (shade: 04 Grey) for CC2
- 1 x pair of 3.75mm knitting needles
- 1 x set of 3.75mm double-pointed needles
- 2 x 15mm buttons
- Tapestry needle
- Toy stuffing

Tension

22 sts and 30 rows to 10cm over st st using 3.75mm needles.

Pattern

Bottom

Using knitting needles and MC, CO 40 sts.

Next row: p to end.

Next row: k2, m1, k to last 2 sts, m1, k2. 42 sts.

* *Next row:* p3, m1p, p to last 3 sts, m1p, p3. 44 sts.

Next row: k2, m1, k to last 2 sts, m1, k2. 46 sts.

Repeat from * once more. 50 sts.

** *Next row:* p to end.

Next row: k2, m1, k to last 2 sts, m1, k2. 52 sts.

Repeat from ** 7 times more. 66 sts.

*** *Next row:* p to end.

Next row: k to end.

Next row: p to end.

Next row: k2, m1, k to last 2 sts, m1, k2. 68 sts.

Repeat from *** twice more. 72 sts.

Work 5 rows straight in st st.

Next row: k2, m1, k to last 2 sts, m1, k2. 74 sts.

Work 7 rows straight in st st.

Next row: k2, ssk, k to last 4 sts, k2tog, k2. 72 sts.

Work 5 rows straight in st st.

Next row: k2, ssk, k to last 4 sts, k2tog, k2. 70 sts.

******Next row:** p to end.

Next row: k to end.

Next row: p to end.

Next row: k2, ssk, k to last 4 sts, k2tog, k2. 68 sts.

Repeat from **** once more. 66 sts.

*******Next row:** p to end.

Next row: k2, ssk, k to last 4 sts, k2tog, k2. 64 sts.

Repeat from ***** 7 times more. 50 sts.

********Next row:** p2, p2tog, p to last 4 sts, p2togtbl, p2. 48 sts.

Next row: k2, ssk, k to last 4 sts, k2tog, k2. 46 sts.

Repeat from ****** once more. 42 sts.

Next row: p2, p2tog, p to last 4 sts, p2togtbl, p2. 40 sts. Cast off all sts.

Top

Using knitting needles and CC1, work as for Back.

Weave in ends and sew front and back together, leaving cast-off edges unsewn.

Spots (make 7)

Using dpns and MC, CO 2 sts.

Next row: [kf&b] x 2. 4 sts.

Put 2 sts each on 2 dpns and use a 3rd dpn to join in the round.

Next round: [kf&b] x 4. 8 sts.

Next round: k to end.

Next round: [kf&b] x 8. 16 sts.

Next round: k to end.

Next round: *k1, kf&b, repeat from * to end. 24 sts.

Next round: k to end.

Repeat the last 2 rounds once more. 36 sts.

Cast off loosely, leaving a long tail. Draw cast-on tail through the centre and weave in this end.

To block Spots and Body, soak in lukewarm water for a few minutes, then lay flat to dry.

Using the tails, sew Spots on Body as pictured.

Legs (make 6)

Using MC and dpns, pick up and k 8 sts along top right edge of RS (CC1 side) of Body. Using a 2nd dpn, turn and pick up and k 8 sts along MC side directly behind the sts you just picked up. Using a 3rd dpn, join to work in the round.

Work in st st for 4cm.

Next round: *k1, kf&b, repeat from * to end. 24 sts.

Work 5 rounds.

Next round: *k1, k2tog, repeat from * to end. 16 sts.

Next round: k to end.

Stuff Leg, ensuring you fill the ball of the foot. Leg can be fairly stiff.

Next round: *k2tog, repeat from * around. 8 sts.

Break yarn and draw it through remaining sts, pulling tight to close the hole. Weave in ends.

Head

Leaving unsewn edge of Body untouched, using dpns and CC2, place a dpn 3cm in from the side and pick up and k 22 sts along top CC1 edge of Body. Using a 2nd dpn, turn and pick up 22 sts along bottom MC side directly behind the sts you just picked up. Divide these sts evenly among your dpns and join to work in the round.

Work in st st for 2cm.

Next round: k4, m1, k14, m1, k to end.

Next round: k6, m1, k12, m1, k to end.

Next round: k8, m1, k10, m1, k to end.

Next round: k10, m1, k8, m1, k to end. 52 sts.

Next round: k to end.

Next round: k9, ssk, k8, k2tog, k to end.

Next round: k9, ssk, k6, k2tog, k to end.

Next round: k9, ssk, k4, k2tog, k to end.

Next round: k9, ssk, k2, k2tog, k to end. 44 sts.

Next round: k to end.

Sew buttons at bumps created by row between the increases and decreases.

Next round: k1, ssk, k16, k2tog, k2, ssk, k16, k2tog, k1. 40 sts.

Next round: k1, ssk, k14, k2tog, k2, ssk, k14, k2tog, k1.

Next round: k1, ssk, k12, k2tog, k2, ssk, k12, k2tog, k1.

Next round: k1, ssk, k10, k2tog, k2, ssk, k10, k2tog, k1.

Next round: k1, ssk, k8, k2tog, k2, ssk, k8, k2tog, k1.

Next round: k1, ssk, k6, k2tog, k2, ssk, k6, k2tog, k1. 20 sts.

Stuff Head, making sure to get up into the bump at the eyes. Head can be fairly stiff.

Divide sts onto 2 dpns and graft together using Kitchener stitch (see page 17).

Antennae (make 2)

Using MC and dpns, pick up and k 3 sts slightly in from the eye and 2cm from cast-on edge as pictured. Using a 2nd dpn, pick up and k 3 sts directly behind the sts you just picked up. Using a 3rd dpn, join to work in the round.

Work in st st for 2cm.

Break yarn and draw it through remaining sts, pulling tight to close the hole.

Finishing

Stuff Body, being careful not to overstuff it. In this case, we want the Body to be soft and squishy and more like a pillow than a ball.

Weave in remaining ends.

Playtime Hot Pad & Mitts

Maile loves her toy kitchen. She cooks me all her favourite meals and even washes up afterwards, and she is very, very careful to ensure she always uses her hot mitts before taking anything out of the oven.

Size

One size

Materials

- 1 x 100g ball Rowan Creative Focus Worsted (shade: 00018 Golden Heather) for MC
- 1 x 100g ball Rowan Creative Focus Worsted (shade: 00410 Espresso) for CC
- 1 x pair of 4.5mm knitting needles for Hot Pad
- 1 x set of 4.5mm double-pointed needles for Hot Mitts and Hot Pad
- Stitch marker
- Spare yarn
- Tapestry Needle

Tension

20 sts and 24 rows to 10cm over st st using 4.5mm needles.

Pattern

Hot Pad

Using knitting needles and MC, CO 21 sts.

Next row: *k1, p1, repeat from * to last st, end k1.

Repeat this row until piece measures 12cm from cast-on edge. Cast off all sts.

Using dpns, pick up and k 21 sts across cast-on edge, 20 sts up left edge, 20 sts across cast-off edge and 19 sts across right edge. 80 sts. Work i-cord edging as follows: CO 3 sts using the cable cast-on method (see page 13), *sl 3 sts from right to left needle, pull yarn around back and k2, p2tog. Repeat from * to last 3 sts, working on the picked-up sts around the edge of the piece.

Work i-cord (see page 14) for 5cm. Break yarn, leaving a long tail. Draw tail through remaining 3 sts and pull tight.

Sew end of i-cord to beginning of i-cord to make a loop. Weave in ends.

Hot Mitts (make 2)

(**Note:** Hot Mitts are worked inside out).

Using dpns and MC, CO 34 sts. Divide sts evenly across dpns, pm and join to work in the round.

Round 1: *k1, p1, repeat from * to end.

Round 2: *p1, k1, repeat from * to end.

Repeat Rounds 1 and 2 (which set moss stitch pattern) 4 times more.

Next round: (work increased sts into pattern when possible, otherwise work them in st st) k1, m1, work 18 sts, m1, work 2 sts, m1, work 18 sts, m1, work 1 st. 38 sts.

Work 10 rounds, keeping moss stitch pattern in place.

Next row: work 1 st, m1, work 20 sts, m1, work 2 sts, m1, work 20 sts, m1, work 1 st. 42 sts.

Next row: work 17 sts, place next 8 sts on spare yarn to hold for Thumb, work to end. 34 sts on needle.

Work 9 rounds, keeping moss stitch pattern in place and bringing sts on either side of held Thumb sts together on first row to continue the round.

Next round: work 1 st, m1, work 15 sts, m1, work 2 sts, m1, work 15 sts, m1, work 1 st. 38 sts.

Work 10 rounds, keeping moss stitch pattern in place.

Next round: work 1 st, ssk, work 13 sts, k2tog, work 2 sts, ssk, work 13 sts, k2tog, work 1 st. 34 sts.

Next round: work 1 round in pattern.

Next round: work 1 st, ssk, work 11 sts, k2tog, work 2 sts, ssk, work 11 sts, k2tog, work 1 st. 30 sts.

Work 1 round straight.

Next round: work 1 st, ssk, work 9 sts, k2tog, work 2 sts, ssk, work 9 sts, k2tog, work 1 st. 26 sts.

Next round: work 1 round in pattern.

Next round: work 1 st, ssk, work 7 sts, k2tog, work 2 sts, ssk, work 7 sts, k2tog, work 1 st. 22 sts.

Cast off all sts using three-needle cast-off method as follows:
Place 1st 11 sts of mitt on one needle and 2nd 11 sts on second needle. Hold the needles parallel in your left hand and insert the tip of a 3rd needle into the 1st st on each of your first 2 needles. K these 2 sts together and pull the 1st st from the parallel needles off. You will have 1 st on the 3rd needle. *Insert the tip of the 3rd needle into the next st on each of the parallel needles. K them together and pull the sts off. You will have 2 sts on the 3rd needle. Using the tip of one of your parallel needles, pull the first worked st on the 3rd needle over the 2nd (just as you normally would when casting off, only your hands are a bit full). Repeat from * until only 1 st remains on the 3rd needle. Break yarn, leaving a long tail. Pull the tail through the remaining st.

Place held Thumb sts on 2 dpns. Using a 3rd dpn, pick up and k 3 sts along the top of thumbhole, pm and join to work in the round.

Work in moss stitch for 6cm. Break yarn, leaving a long tail. Thread the end of the tail onto the tapestry needle. Pull yarn tightly through remaining sts and tie a knot. Weave in all ends on the outside, then flip mitt inside out. The RS is now facing.

Using CC, pick up and k 34 sts along cast-on edge (cuff).

Work i-cord edging as follows:
CO 3 sts using the cable cast-on method (see page 12), *sl 3 sts from right to left needle. Pull yarn around back and k2, p2tog. Repeat from * until 3 sts remain. Work i-cord (see page 14) for 5cm. Break yarn, leaving a long tail. Draw the tail through the remaining 3 sts and pull tight.

Sew end of i-cord to beginning of i-cord to make a loop. Weave in ends.

Lily Beret

This sweet and stylish little beret is easy to make, providing a good introduction to knitting lace, if you're not too familiar with it. It's the perfect accessory for a spring day that has just a bit of chill in the air.

Sizes

12–24 months (2T–3T, 4T) (shown in 4T)

Materials

- 1 x 100g skein Madelinetosh Tosh Merino Light (shade: 109 Cherry)
- 1 x 3.5mm 30cm circular needle
- 1 x set of 3.5mm double-pointed needles

Tension

26.5 sts and 35.5 rows to 10cm over st st using 3.5mm needles.

Pattern

Using circular needle CO 88 (96, 104) sts, join to work in the round.

Round 1: *k1, p1, repeat from * to end.

Round 2: *p1, k1, repeat from * to end.

Repeat Rounds 1 and 2 4 times more.

Next round: *k4, m1, repeat from * to end. 110 (120, 130) sts.

Work in st st for 7cm (8cm, 9cm).

Sizes 12–24 months and 2–3T only

Increase 2 (8) sts evenly across round. 112 (128) sts.

Size 4T only

Decrease 2 sts evenly. 128 sts.

All sizes

Begin working flower as follows:

Round 1: k6, *yf, sl 1-k2tog-psso, yf, k13, repeat from * to last 10 sts, yf, sl 1-k2tog-psso, yf, k7.

Round 2: k to end.

Round 3: k5, *yf, k1, sl 1-k2tog-psso, k1, yf, k11, repeat from * to last 11 sts, yf, k1, sl 1-k2tog-psso, k1, yf, k6.

Round 4: k to end.

Round 5: k4, *yf, k2, sl 1-k2tog-psso, k2, yf, k9, repeat from * to last 12 sts, yf, k2, sl 1-k2tog-psso, k2, yf, k5.

Round 6: k to end.

Round 7: k3, *yf, k3, sl 1-k2tog-psso, k3, yf, k7, repeat from * to last 13 sts, yf, k3, sl 1-k2tog-psso, k3, yf, k4.

Round 8: k to end.

Round 9: k2, *yf, k4, sl 1-k2tog-psso, k4, yf, k5, repeat from * to last 14 sts, yf, k4, sl 1-k2tog-psso, k4, yf, k3.

Round 10: k to end.

Round 11: k1, *yf, k5, sl 1-k2tog-psso, k5, yf, k3, repeat from * to last 15 sts, yf, k5, sl 1-k2tog-psso, k5, yf, k2.

Round 12: k to end.

Round 13: *yf, k6, sl 1-k2tog-psso, k6, yf, k1, repeat from * to end.

Round 14: k to end.

Round 15: as Round 13.

Round 16: k to end.

Round 17: *yf, ssk, k4, sl 1-k2tog-psso, k4, k2tog, yf, k1, repeat from * to end. 102 (112, 112) sts.

Round 18: k to end.

Round 19: *yf, ssk, k3, sl 1-k2tog-psso, k3, k2tog, yf, k1, repeat from * to end. 88 (96, 96) sts.

Round 20: k to end.

Round 21: *yf, ssk, k2, sl 1-k2tog-psso, k2, k2tog, yf, k1, repeat from * to end. 74 (80, 80) sts.

Round 22: k to end.

Round 23: *yf, ssk, k1, sl 1-k2tog-psso, k1, k2tog, yf, k1, repeat from * to end. 60 (64, 64) sts.

Round 24: k to end.

Round 25: *yf, ssk, sl 1-k2tog-psso, k2tog, yf, k1, repeat from * to end. 46 (48, 48) sts.

Round 26: k to end.

Round 27: k1, * sl 1-k2tog-psso, k3, repeat from * to last 5 sts, end sl 1-k2tog-psso, k2. 32 sts.

Round 28: *k2tog, repeat from * to end. 16 sts.

Round 29: *k2tog, repeat from * to end. 8 sts.

Round 30: *k2tog, repeat from * to end. 4 sts.

Work i-cord (see page 14) for 1cm. Break yarn, leaving a long tail. Draw it through remaining sts and pull tight.

Finishing
Weave in ends. To block, soak beret in lukewarm water for a few minutes, then stretch over a dinner plate. Stretch out flower so it lies flat and leave beret to dry.

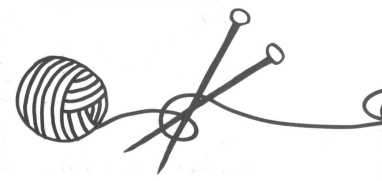

Index

Acknowledgements

Thank you so much to Catharine Robertson for all her hard work and flexibility, and to Judith Hannam and Kyle Cathie and everyone at Kyle Books. This beautiful book would not be nearly so gorgeous without Ali Allen's wonderful photographs, or without the spectacular design by Laura Woussen. It would also be senseless without the efforts of Salima Hirani and Katie Hardwicke.

Thank you to my blog readers, and my dear test knitters without whom I would be utterly lost. Thank you to Mia Rosa for her beautiful Keaton Cardigan and Joseph Cardigan. Thank you to Patricia's Yarns, to Do Ewe Knit, and to 2 Stix and a String. Thank you to Jen Hughes for encouragement and babysitting, and thank you to all of Maile's friends and relations for being so inspiring!

Thank you Mom and Dad, and thank you Dave for really, really trying to respond in a thoughtful manner to questions like, 'What do you think of this stitch pattern?'. Thank you to Maile for being willing to try everything on and be measured and photographed and generally poked and prodded. Thank you for being you. I love you all.